Weekday Eucharistic Propers 2015

Church Publishing
NEW YORK

Copyright © 2017 by The Domestic and Foreign Missionary Society of The Protestant Episcopal Church in the United States of America

Portions of this book may be reproduced by a congregation for its own use. Commercial or large-scale reproduction for sale of any portion of this book or of the book as a whole, without the written permission of Church Publishing Incorporated, is prohibited.

Cover design and typesetting by Linda Brooks

ISBN-13: 978-1-64065-078-7 (pbk.)
ISBN-13: 978-1-64065-079-4 (ebook)

Church Publishing, Incorporated.
19 East 34th Street
New York, New York 10016

www.churchpublishing.org

Contents

1. Introduction: Weekday Eucharists and the Calendar   1

2. The Temporal Cycle: Seasons of the church year   3
    Weekdays of Advent and Christmas until the Baptism of Christ   5
    Weekdays of Lent   12
    Holy Week   46
    Easter Week   52
    Weekdays of Easter   58
    Ordinary Time (the Seasons after Epiphany and Pentecost):
        A Two-Year Weekday Eucharistic Lectionary   76
    Six-Week Lectionary with Themes and Collects   111

3. The Sanctoral Cycle: Commemorations of Saints   118
    Common of Saints from the Book of Common Prayer   121
    New Commons of Saints   136

4. Various Occasions   142
    Various Occasions from the Book of Common Prayer   144
    New Propers for Various Occasions   175

1. Introduction:
Weekday Eucharists and the Calendar

In the section entitled "Concerning the Service of the Church," the Book of Common Prayer identifies the normative services of the Episcopal Church:

> The Holy Eucharist, the principal act of Christian worship on the Lord's Day and other major Feasts, and Daily Morning and Evening Prayer, as set forth in this book, are the regular services appointed for public worship in the Church. (BCP, 13)

Eucharistic propers (collects, Scripture readings, and proper prefaces) are provided in the Book of Common Prayer for the days when the Eucharist is the principal service. The Calendar section at the front of the Prayer Book identifies these eucharistic feasts by placing them into three categories, ranked by priority: Principal Feasts, Sundays, and Holy Days. Normatively, on all other days, Morning and Evening Prayer are the Church's official public services. However, as celebration of the Eucharist has become more frequent, many congregations and other communities of faith now celebrate weekday Eucharists on days for which the Prayer Book does not assign propers.

The Prayer Book provides a range of possible options for the celebration of the Eucharist on these ferial or non-feast days. These options include the celebration of:

- a Major Feast that has fallen elsewhere in the week (BCP, 17);
- a commemoration listed in the Calendar (BCP, 18);
- a commemoration not appointed in the Church's Calendar by using the Common of Saints (BCP, 18);
- an Ember Day or Rogation Day (BCP, 18);

- the season, by using the propers of the preceding Sunday (BCP, 158);
- the weekdays of Holy Week and Easter, by using the propers appointed in the Book of Common Prayer;
- an occasion provided for in the propers for Various Occasions (BCP, 18).

In addition, since 1979 *Lesser Feasts and Fasts* has appointed weekday propers for seasons of the church year.

To facilitate the use of these authorized options, this resource contains weekday propers for the seasons of the church year (the temporal cycle), the Common of Saints (the sanctoral cycle), and Various Occasions from the Prayer Book and from resources authorized since the adoption of the Prayer Book. The propers in this resource are grouped into three sections by type for the temporal cycle, the sanctoral cycle, and various occasions.

Directions for the appropriate use of the various kinds of propers are provided at the head of each section. Here are some general guides for use:

- These propers are not intended for use on Principal Feasts, Sundays, and Holy Days (BCP, 15–17).
- If a Major Feast that falls in the week will not be celebrated with a Eucharist on its indicated day, it is most appropriate that a midweek service observe the Major Feast in order to retain the Prayer Book's emphasis on the significance of these occasions.
- "Feasts appointed on fixed days in the Calendar are not observed on the days of Holy Week or of Easter Week," nor are propers for Various Occasions used within this period (BCP, 18).
- In keeping with ancient tradition, the observance of Lenten weekdays ordinarily takes precedence over Lesser Feasts occurring during this season.
- Since the triumphs of the saints are a continuation and manifestation of the Paschal victory of Christ, the celebration of saints' days is particularly appropriate during the Easter season.

The 2015 General Convention authorized this liturgical resource to make readily available a variety of options for weekday celebrations of the Eucharist.

2. The Temporal Cycle: Seasons of the church year

Introduction

The mid-twentieth-century liturgical renewal movement made a great impact on the liturgical reforms of the Roman Catholic Second Vatican Council and on the subsequent revisions of many Western families of Christianity, including the Episcopal Church and our Book of Common Prayer. In reaching back to the ancient foundations of Christian liturgy, the liturgical renewal movement reminded the Church universal of the vital importance of Sundays as the primordial feast day and the weekly feast of Christ's resurrection.

As Sundays have become more central, the seasons of the church year—the temporal cycle—have become correspondingly more important. The celebration of seasonal ferial days with weekday celebrations of the Eucharist is a way to reinforce the importance of Sundays and seasons within the local congregation.

It is appropriate to use the propers appointed for Sunday or a Principal Feast through the rest of the following week. However, in places where weekday eucharistic services are frequent, this practice can become repetitive. In order to retain the emphasis on the temporal cycle yet still provide rich fodder for spiritual reflection and growth, a weekday eucharistic lectionary with seasonally appropriate scriptural texts is provided here. The seasons of Lent and Easter are provided with a number of collects for the weekdays; in other seasons, the collect remains as appointed on the preceding Sunday or Principal Feast, as the Prayer Book directs.

The weekday eucharistic lectionary offered here is adapted from the weekday eucharistic lectionary used in the Roman Catholic Church and the Anglican Church of Canada. This scheme provides one set of readings for the seasons of Advent, Christmas, Lent, and Easter. Two sets of readings are provided for the seasons after Epiphany and after Pentecost (sometimes referred to as "Ordinary Time"), to be used in alternating years: Year 1 is used in odd-numbered years, and Year 2 in even-numbered years.

Additionally, a set of alternate six-week thematic readings suitable for use in Ordinary Time (first authorized by the 1994 General Convention) is located after the presentation of the sequential scheme.

The Daily Office and the Temporal Cycle

The Daily Office is rooted in the movement of the temporal cycle; this cycle is its natural habitat. In particular, the principle of the continuous reading of Scripture is only enacted when the temporal cycle is followed. Too many interruptions lose the thread of the sacred narratives and prevent the formative encounter with Scripture that has been an historic gift of this discipline.

Only Major Feasts are intended to alter the Daily Office lectionary cycle. The readings found in the Common of Saints and the Propers for Various Occasions are for use at the Eucharist or for devotional reading, and are not intended to displace the appointed daily reading.

Some worshiping communities regularly use the Sunday collect as the Collect of the Day in the Office through the subsequent week. The repetition helps secure the seasonal themes and perspectives in the mind of the Church. When a sanctoral collect is used in the Office as the Collect of the Day, the temporal collect of the preceding Sunday or Principal Feast may be used after the Collect of the Day in order to maintain a connection with the Church's seasons.

Weekdays of Advent and Christmas until the Baptism of Christ

Concerning the Proper

Proper Lessons and Psalms are provided for the Eucharist for the weekdays of Advent and Christmas to the First Sunday after Epiphany. These Propers are also suitable for use at Liturgies of the Word held on those days.

During the weeks of Advent 1 through 3, the first Readings from Isaiah point to the coming of God's reign. In the fourth week of Advent, the first Readings are in thematic harmony with the Gospel lections and reflect on the sacred history of God's people in light of God's coming reign.

The Gospel Readings for the first three weeks of Advent point to Jesus' words and acts as fulfilling the expectations of God's coming reign. Lections for the fourth week are taken from the first two chapters of Matthew and Luke and prepare the Church for the Christmas celebration. The first Readings for the weekdays following Christmas Day provide a sequential reading of the First Letter of John, which reflects on the significance of Jesus' life for the Church. The Gospel lections recall the early events of Jesus' life and the beginning of his ministry that revealed his authority and power.

Any of the Readings may be lengthened at discretion, and the selections from the Psalter may be lengthened or shortened.

Where there is not a daily celebration of the Eucharist, the Proper appointed for any weekday may be used on any other weekday in the same week.

On days of optional observance on the Calendar, the Collect, Lessons, Psalm and Preface are ordinarily those of the saint. Where there is a daily celebration, however, the weekday Lessons and Psalm may be substituted.

The Collect of the previous Sunday may be used on ordinary weekdays, except that the third collect for the Nativity of Our Lord: Christmas Day is used for any weekdays between Holy Innocents' Day and the First Sunday after Christmas Day. Any of the sets of Proper Lessons for Christmas Day may serve for any weekdays between Holy Innocents' Day and the First Sunday after Christmas Day.

The First Week of Advent

	Psalms	Lessons
Monday	122	Isaiah 2:1–5 (*or* in Year A, Isaiah 4:2–6) Matthew 8:5–13
Tuesday	72:1–8	Isaiah 11:1–10 Luke 10:21–24
Wednesday	23	Isaiah 25:6–9 Matthew 15:29–39
Thursday	118:19–24	Isaiah 26:1–6 Matthew 7:21–27
Friday	27:1–6,17–18	Isaiah 29:17–24 Matthew 9:27–31
Saturday	147:1–12	Isaiah 30:19–21,23–26 Matthew 9:35–10:1,5–8

The Second Week of Advent

	Psalms	Lessons
Monday	85:8–13	Isaiah 35:1–10 Luke 5:17–26
Tuesday	96 (*or* in Year B, 50:7–15)	Isaiah 40:1–11 (*or* in Year B, Amos 5:18–24) Matthew 18:12–14
Wednesday	103:1–10	Isaiah 40:25–31 Matthew 11:28–30
Thursday	145:1–4,8–13	Isaiah 41:13–20 Matthew 11:7–15
Friday	1	Isaiah 48:17–19 Matthew 11:16–19
Saturday	80:1–3,14–18	Sirach 48:1–11 Matthew 17:9–13

The Third Week of Advent

	Psalms	Lessons
Monday	25:3–8	Numbers 24:2–7,15–17a Matthew 21:23–27
Tuesday	34:1–8	Zephaniah 3:1–2,9–13 Matthew 21:28–32
Wednesday	85:8–13	Isaiah 45:5–8(9–17)18–25 Luke 7:19–23
Thursday	30	Isaiah 54:1–10 Luke 7:24–30
Friday	67	Isaiah 56:1–8 John 5:33–36

December 17 – December 24

	Psalms	Lessons
17	72:1–8	Genesis 49:2,8–10 Matthew 1:1–7,17
18	72:11–18	Jeremiah 23:5–8 Matthew 1:18–25
19	71:1–8	Judges 13:2–7,24–25 Luke 1:5–25
20	24	Isaiah 7:10–14 Luke 1:26–38
21	33:1–5,20–22	Zephaniah 3:14–18a (*or* in Year C, Song of Solomon 2:8–14) Luke 1:39–45
22	Canticle 9 *or* 113 *or* 122	1 Samuel 1:19–28 Luke 1:46–56
23	25:1–14	Malachi 3:1–5 Luke 1:57–66
24	89:1–4,19–29	2 Samuel 7:1–16 Luke 1:67–79

December 26 – December 31

	Psalms	Lessons
26	Collect and Proper Lessons for St. Stephen	
27	Collect and Proper Lessons for St. John	
28	Collect and Proper Lessons for the Holy Innocents	
29	96:1–9	1 John 2:7–11 Luke 2:22–35
30	96:7–10	1 John 2:12–17 Luke 2:36–40
31	96:1–2, 11–13	1 John 2:18–21 John 1:1–18

January 2 – January 12

	Psalms	Lessons
2	98:1–5	1 John 2:22–29 John 1:19–28
3	98:1–2,4–7	1 John 3:1–6 John 1:29–34
4	98:1–2,8–10	1 John 3:7–10 John 1:35–42
5	100	1 John 3:11–18 John 1:43–51
7	2	1 John 3:18–4:6 Matthew 4:12–17,23–25
8	72:1–8	1 John 4:7–12 Mark 6:30–44
9	72:1–2,10–13	1 John 4:11–19 Mark 6:45–52
10	72:1–2,14–19	1 John 4:19–5:4 Luke 4:14–22
11	147:13–21	1 John 5:5–12 Luke 5:12–16
12	149:1–4	1 John 5:13–21 John 3:22–30

The Monday after the Baptism of Christ begins Ordinary Time, the Weeks after Epiphany.

Weekdays of Lent

Concerning the Proper

Proper Collects, Lessons, and Psalms are provided for the Eucharist on the weekdays of Lent. These Propers are also suitable for use at Liturgies of the Word (preaching services) held on those days. The First Lesson is invariably from the Old Testament, and is chosen to match the appointed Gospel.

Any of the Readings may be lengthened at discretion. Suggested lengthenings are shown in parentheses. The selections from the Psalter may be lengthened or shortened.

Where there is not a daily celebration of the Eucharist, the Proper appointed for any weekday may be used on any other weekday in the same week.

In keeping with ancient tradition, the observance of Lenten weekdays ordinarily takes precedence over Lesser Feasts occurring during this season. It is appropriate, however, to name the saint whose day it is in the Prayers of the People, and, if desired, to use the Collect of the saint to conclude the Prayers.

Thursday after Ash Wednesday

I   Direct us, O Lord, in all our doings with thy most gracious favor, and further us with thy continual help; that in all our works begun, continued, and ended in thee, we may glorify thy holy Name, and finally, by thy mercy, obtain everlasting life; through Jesus Christ our Lord, who liveth and reigneth with thee and the Holy Spirit, one God, for ever and ever. *Amen.*

II Direct us, O Lord, in all our doings with your most gracious favor, and further us with your continual help; that in all our works begun, continued, and ended in you, we may glorify your holy Name, and finally, by your mercy, obtain everlasting life; through Jesus Christ our Lord, who lives and reigns with you and the Holy Spirit, one God, for ever and ever. *Amen.*

Psalm	Lessons
1	Deuteronomy 30:15–20
	Luke 9:18–25

Preface of Lent

Friday after Ash Wednesday

I Support us, O Lord, with thy gracious favor through the fast we have begun; that as we observe it by bodily self-denial, so we may fulfill it with inner sincerity of heart; through Jesus Christ our Lord, who liveth and reigneth with thee and the Holy Spirit, one God, for ever and ever. *Amen.*

II Support us, O Lord, with your gracious favor through the fast we have begun; that as we observe it by bodily self-denial, so we may fulfill it with inner sincerity of heart; through Jesus Christ our Lord, who lives and reigns with you and the Holy Spirit, one God, for ever and ever. *Amen.*

Psalm	Lessons
51:1–10	Isaiah 58:1–9a
	Matthew 9:10–17

Preface of Lent

Saturday after Ash Wednesday

I   Almighty and everlasting God, mercifully look upon our infirmities, and in all our dangers and necessities stretch forth thy right hand to help and defend us; through Jesus Christ our Lord, who liveth and reigneth with thee and the Holy Spirit, one God, for ever and ever. *Amen.*

II Almighty and everlasting God, mercifully look upon our infirmities, and in all our dangers and necessities stretch forth your right hand to help and defend us; through Jesus Christ our Lord, who lives and reigns with you and the Holy Spirit, one God, for ever and ever. *Amen.*

Psalm	Lessons
86:1–11	Isaiah 58:9b-14
	Luke 5:27–32

Preface of Lent

Monday in the First Week of Lent

I   Almighty and everlasting God, mercifully increase in us thy gifts of holy discipline, in almsgiving, prayer, and fasting; that our lives may be directed to the fulfilling of thy most gracious will; through Jesus Christ our Lord, who liveth and reigneth with thee and the Holy Spirit, one God, for ever and ever. *Amen.*

II   Almighty and everlasting God, mercifully increase in us your gifts of holy discipline, in almsgiving, prayer, and fasting; that our lives may be directed to the fulfilling of your most gracious will; through Jesus Christ our Lord, who lives and reigns with you and the Holy Spirit, one God, for ever and ever. *Amen.*

Psalm	Lessons
19:7–14	Leviticus 19:1–2,11–18
	Matthew 25:31–46

Preface of Lent

Tuesday in the First Week of Lent

I Grant to thy people, Lord, grace to withstand the temptations of the world, the flesh, and the devil, and with pure hearts and minds to follow thee, the only true God; through Jesus Christ thy Son our Lord, who liveth and reigneth with thee and the Holy Spirit, one God, for ever and ever. *Amen.*

II Grant to your people, Lord, grace to withstand the temptations of the world, the flesh, and the devil, and with pure hearts and minds to follow you, the only true God; through Jesus Christ your Son our Lord, who lives and reigns with you and the Holy Spirit, one God, for ever and ever. *Amen.*

Psalm	Lessons
34:15–22	Isaiah 55:6–11
	Matthew 6:7–15

Preface of Lent

Wednesday in the First Week of Lent

I Bless us, O God, in this holy season, in which our hearts seek thy help and healing; and so purify us by thy discipline that we may grow in grace and in the knowledge of our Lord and Savior Jesus Christ; who liveth and reigneth with thee and the Holy Spirit, one God, for ever and ever. *Amen.*

II Bless us, O God, in this holy season, in which our hearts seek your help and healing; and so purify us by your discipline that we may grow in grace and in the knowledge of our Lord and Savior Jesus Christ; who lives and reigns with you and the Holy Spirit, one God, for ever and ever. *Amen.*

Psalm	**Lessons**
51:11–18	Jonah 3:1–10
	Luke 11:29–32

Preface of Lent

Thursday in the First Week of Lent

I Strengthen us, O Lord, by thy grace, that in thy might we may overcome all spiritual enemies, and with pure hearts serve thee; through Jesus Christ our Lord, who liveth and reigneth with thee and the Holy Spirit, one God, for ever and ever. *Amen.*

II Strengthen us, O Lord, by your grace, that in your might we may overcome all spiritual enemies, and with pure hearts serve you; through Jesus Christ our Lord, who lives and reigns with you and the Holy Spirit, one God, for ever and ever. *Amen.*

Psalm	**Lessons**
138	Esther (Apocrypha) 14:1–6,12–14
	Matthew 7:7–12

Preface of Lent

Friday in the First Week of Lent

I Lord Christ, our eternal Redeemer, grant us such fellowship in thy sufferings, that, filled with thy Holy Spirit, we may subdue the flesh to the spirit, and the spirit to thee, and at the last attain to the glory of thy resurrection; who livest and reignest with the Father and the Holy Spirit, one God, for ever and ever. *Amen.*

II Lord Christ, our eternal Redeemer, grant us such fellowship in your sufferings, that, filled with your Holy Spirit, we may subdue the flesh to the spirit, and the spirit to you, and at the last attain to the glory of your resurrection; who lives and reigns with the Father and the Holy Spirit, one God, for ever and ever. *Amen.*

Psalm	Lessons
130	Ezekiel 18:21–28
	Matthew 5:20–26

Preface of Lent

Saturday in the First Week of Lent

I O God, who by thy Word dost marvelously carry out the work of reconciliation: Grant that in our Lenten fast we may be devoted to thee with all our hearts, and united with one another in prayer and holy love; through Jesus Christ our Lord, who liveth and reigneth with thee and the Holy Spirit, one God, for ever and ever. *Amen.*

II O God, by your Word you marvelously carry out the work of reconciliation: Grant that in our Lenten fast we may be devoted to you with all our hearts, and united with one another in prayer and holy love; through Jesus Christ our Lord, who lives and reigns with you and the Holy Spirit, one God, for ever and ever. *Amen.*

Psalm	Lessons
119:1–8	Deuteronomy 26:16–19 Matthew 5:43–48

Preface of Lent

Monday in the Second Week of Lent

I   Let thy Spirit, O Lord, come into the midst of us to wash us with the pure water of repentance, and prepare us to be always a living sacrifice unto thee; through Jesus Christ our Lord, who liveth and reigneth with thee and the Holy Spirit, one God, for ever and ever. *Amen.*

II Let your Spirit, O Lord, come into the midst of us to wash us with the pure water of repentance, and prepare us to be always a living sacrifice to you; through Jesus Christ our Lord, who lives and reigns with you and the Holy Spirit, one God, for ever and ever. *Amen.*

Psalm	Lessons
79:1–9	Daniel 9:3–10 Luke 6:27–38

Preface of Lent

Tuesday in the Second Week of Lent

I O God, who didst will to redeem us from all iniquity by thy Son: Deliver us when we are tempted to regard sin without abhorrence, and let the virtue of his passion come between us and our mortal enemy; through Jesus Christ our Lord, who liveth and reigneth with thee and the Holy Spirit, one God, for ever and ever. *Amen.*

II O God, you willed to redeem us from all iniquity by your Son: Deliver us when we are tempted to regard sin without abhorrence, and let the virtue of his passion come between us and our mortal enemy; through Jesus Christ our Lord, who lives and reigns with you and the Holy Spirit, one God, for ever and ever. *Amen.*

Psalm	Lessons
50:7–15,22–24	Isaiah 1:2–4,16–20
	Matthew 23:1–12

Preface of Lent

Wednesday in the Second Week of Lent

I O God, who didst so love the world that thou gavest thine only-begotten Son to reconcile earth with heaven: Grant that we, loving thee above all things, may love our friends in thee, and our enemies for thy sake; through Jesus Christ our Lord, who liveth and reigneth with thee and the Holy Spirit, one God, for ever and ever. *Amen.*

II O God, you so loved the world that you gave your only begotten Son to reconcile earth with heaven: Grant that we, loving you above all things, may love our friends in you, and our enemies for your sake; through Jesus Christ our Lord, who lives and reigns with you and the Holy Spirit, one God, for ever and ever. *Amen.*

Psalm	Lessons
31:9–16	Jeremiah 18:1–11,18–20
	Matthew 20:17–28

Preface of Lent

Thursday in the Second Week of Lent

I O Lord, strong and mighty, Lord of hosts and King of glory: Cleanse our hearts from sin, keep our hands pure, and turn our minds from what is passing away; so that at the last we may stand in thy holy place and receive thy blessing; through Jesus Christ our Lord, who liveth and reigneth with thee and the Holy Spirit, one God, for ever and ever. *Amen.*

II O Lord, strong and mighty, Lord of hosts and King of glory: Cleanse our hearts from sin, keep our hands pure, and turn our minds from what is passing away; so that at the last we may stand in your holy place and receive your blessing; through Jesus Christ our Lord, who lives and reigns with you and the Holy Spirit, one God, for ever and ever. *Amen.*

Psalm	Lessons
1	Jeremiah 17:5–10
	Luke 16:19–31

Preface of Lent

Friday in the Second Week of Lent

I Grant, O Lord, that as thy Son Jesus Christ prayed for his enemies on the cross, so we may have grace to forgive those who wrongfully or scornfully use us, that we ourselves may be able to receive thy forgiveness; through Jesus Christ our Lord, who liveth and reigneth with thee and the Holy Spirit, one God, for ever and ever. *Amen.*

II Grant, O Lord, that as your Son Jesus Christ prayed for his enemies on the cross, so we may have grace to forgive those who wrongfully or scornfully use us, that we ourselves may be able to receive your forgiveness; through Jesus Christ our Lord, who lives and reigns with you and the Holy Spirit, one God, for ever and ever. *Amen.*

Psalm	Lessons
105:16–22	Genesis 37:3–4,12–28
	Matthew 21:33–43

Preface of Lent

Saturday in the Second Week of Lent

I Grant, most merciful Lord, to thy faithful people pardon and peace, that they may be cleansed from all their sins, and serve thee with a quiet mind; through Jesus Christ our Lord, who liveth and reigneth with thee and the Holy Spirit, one God, for ever and ever. *Amen.*

II Grant, most merciful Lord, to your faithful people pardon and peace, that they may be cleansed from all their sins, and serve you with a quiet mind; through Jesus Christ our Lord, who lives and reigns with you and the Holy Spirit, one God, for ever and ever. *Amen.*

Psalm	Lessons
103:1–4(5–8)9–12	Micah 7:14–15,18–20
	Luke 15:11–32

Preface of Lent

Monday in the Third Week of Lent

I Look upon the hearty desires of thy humble servants, we beseech thee, Almighty God, and stretch forth the right hand of thy majesty to be our defense against all our enemies; through Jesus Christ our Lord, who liveth and reigneth with thee and the Holy Spirit, one God, for ever and ever. *Amen.*

II Look upon the heart-felt desires of your humble servants, Almighty God, and stretch forth the right hand of your majesty to be our defense against all our enemies; through Jesus Christ our Lord, who lives and reigns with you and the Holy Spirit, one God, for ever and ever. *Amen.*

Psalm	Lessons
42:1–7	2 Kings 5:1–15b Luke 4:23–30d

Another Proper

The following Psalm and Lessons may be used on any weekday in this week (third week of Lent), especially in Years B and C.

95:6–11	Exodus 17:1–7 John 4:5–26(27–38)39–42

Preface of Lent

Tuesday in the Third Week of Lent

I O Lord, we beseech thee mercifully to hear us; and grant that we, to whom thou hast given a hearty desire to pray, may, by thy mighty aid, be defended and comforted in all dangers and adversities; through Jesus Christ our Lord, who liveth and reigneth with thee and the Holy Spirit, one God, for ever and ever. *Amen.*

II O Lord, we beseech you mercifully to hear us; and grant that we, to whom you have given a fervent desire to pray, may, by your mighty aid, be defended and comforted in all dangers and adversities; through Jesus Christ our Lord, who lives and reigns with you and the Holy Spirit, one God, for ever and ever. *Amen.*

Psalm	**Lessons**
25:3–10	Song of the Three Young Men 2–4,11–20a*
	Matthew 18:21–35

Preface of Lent

* *In some Bibles, Daniel 3:25–27,34–43*

Wednesday in the Third Week of Lent

I Give ear to our prayers, O Lord, and dispose the way of thy servants in safety under thy protection, that, amidst all the changes of our earthly pilgrimage, we may ever be guarded by thy mighty aid; through Jesus Christ our Lord, who liveth and reigneth with thee and the Holy Spirit, one God, for ever and ever. *Amen.*

II Give ear to our prayers, O Lord, and direct the way of your servants in safety under your protection, that, amid all the changes of our earthly pilgrimage, we may be guarded by your mighty aid; through Jesus Christ our Lord, who lives and reigns with you and the Holy Spirit, one God, for ever and ever. *Amen.*

Psalm	Lessons
78:1–6	Deuteronomy 4:1–2,5–9
	Matthew 5:17–19

Preface of Lent

Thursday in the Third Week of Lent

I   Keep watch over thy Church, O Lord, with thine unfailing love; and, seeing that it is grounded in human weakness and cannot maintain itself without thine aid, protect it from all danger, and keep it in the way of salvation; through Jesus Christ thy Son our Lord, who liveth and reigneth with thee and the Holy Spirit, one God, for ever and ever. *Amen.*

II Keep watch over your Church, O Lord, with your unfailing love; and, since it is grounded in human weakness and cannot maintain itself without your aid, protect it from all danger, and keep it in the way of salvation; through Jesus Christ your Son our Lord, who lives and reigns with you and the Holy Spirit, one God, for ever and ever. *Amen.*

Psalm	Lessons
95:6–11	Jeremiah 7:23–28
	Luke 11:14–23

Preface of Lent

Friday in the Third Week of Lent

I Grant us, O Lord our Strength, to have a true love of thy holy Name; that, trusting in thy grace, we may fear no earthly evil, nor fix our hearts on earthly goods, but may rejoice in thy full salvation; through Jesus Christ our Lord, who liveth and reigneth with thee and the Holy Spirit, one God, for ever and ever. *Amen.*

II Grant us, O Lord our Strength, a true love of your holy Name; so that, trusting in your grace, we may fear no earthly evil, nor fix our hearts on earthly goods, but may rejoice in your full salvation; through Jesus Christ our Lord, who lives and reigns with you and the Holy Spirit, one God, for ever and ever. *Amen.*

Psalm	**Lessons**
81:8–14	Hosea 14:1–9
	Mark 12:28–34

Preface of Lent

Saturday in the Third Week of Lent

I O God, who knowest us to be set in the midst of so many and great dangers, that by reason of the frailty of our nature we cannot always stand upright: Grant to us such strength and protection as may support us in all dangers, and carry us through all temptations; through Jesus Christ our Lord, who liveth and reigneth with thee and the Holy Spirit, one God, for ever and ever. *Amen.*

II O God, you know us to be set in the midst of so many and great dangers, that by reason of the frailty of our nature we cannot always stand upright: Grant us such strength and protection as may support us in all dangers, and carry us through all temptations; through Jesus Christ our Lord, who lives and reigns with you and the Holy Spirit, one God, for ever and ever. *Amen.*

Psalm	**Lessons**
51:15–20	Hosea 6:1–6
	Luke 18:9–14

Preface of Lent

Monday in the Fourth Week of Lent

I O Lord our God, who in thy holy Sacraments hast given us a foretaste of the good things of thy kingdom: Direct us, we beseech thee, in the way that leadeth unto eternal life, that we may come to appear before thee in that place of light where thou dost dwell for ever with thy saints; through Jesus Christ our Lord, who liveth and reigneth with thee and the Holy Spirit, one God, for ever and ever. *Amen.*

II O Lord our God, in your holy Sacraments you have given us a foretaste of the good things of your kingdom: Direct us, we pray, in the way that leads to eternal life, that we may come to appear before you in that place of light where you dwell for ever with your saints; through Jesus Christ our Lord, who lives and reigns with you and the Holy Spirit, one God, for ever and ever. *Amen.*

Psalm	**Lessons**
30:1–6,11–13	Isaiah 65:17–25
	John 4:43–54

Another Proper

The following Psalm and Lessons may be used on any weekday in this week (fourth week of Lent), especially in Years B and C.

27:1,10–18	Micah 7:7–9
	John 9:1–13(14–27)28–38

Preface of Lent

Tuesday in the Fourth Week of Lent

I O God, with whom is the well of life, and in whose light we see light: Quench our thirst, we pray thee, with living water, and flood our darkened minds with heavenly light; through Jesus Christ our Lord, who liveth and reigneth with thee and the Holy Spirit, one God, for ever and ever. *Amen.*

II O God, with you is the well of life, and in your light we see light: Quench our thirst with living water, and flood our darkened minds with heavenly light; through Jesus Christ our Lord, who lives and reigns with you and the Holy Spirit, one God, for ever and ever. *Amen.*

Psalm	Lessons
46:1–8	Ezekiel 47:1–9,12
	John 5:1–18

Preface of Lent

Wednesday in the Fourth Week of Lent

I O Lord our God, who didst sustain thine ancient people in the wilderness with bread from heaven: Feed now thy pilgrim flock with the food that endureth unto everlasting life; through Jesus Christ thy Son our Lord, who liveth and reigneth with thee and the Holy Spirit, one God, for ever and ever. *Amen.*

II O Lord our God, you sustained your ancient people in the wilderness with bread from heaven: Feed now your pilgrim flock with the food that endures to everlasting life; through Jesus Christ your Son our Lord, who lives and reigns with you and the Holy Spirit, one God, for ever and ever. *Amen.*

Psalm	Lessons
145:8–19	Isaiah 49:8–15
	John 5:19–29

Preface of Lent

Thursday in the Fourth Week of Lent

I   Almighty and most merciful God, drive from us all weakness of body, mind, and spirit; that, being restored to wholeness, we may with free hearts become what thou dost intend us to be and accomplish what thou willest us to do; through Jesus Christ our Lord, who liveth and reigneth with thee and the Holy Spirit, one God, for ever and ever. *Amen.*

II Almighty and most merciful God, drive from us all weakness of body, mind, and spirit; that, being restored to wholeness, we may with free hearts become what you intend us to be and accomplish what you want us to do; through Jesus Christ our Lord, who lives and reigns with you and the Holy Spirit, one God, for ever and ever. *Amen.*

Psalm

106:6–7,19–23

Lessons

Exodus 32:7–14
John 5:30–47

Preface of Lent

Friday in the Fourth Week of Lent

I O God, who hast given us the Good News of thine abounding love in thy Son Jesus Christ: So fill our hearts with thankfulness that we may rejoice to tell abroad the good tidings we have received; through Jesus Christ our Lord, who liveth and reigneth with thee and the Holy Spirit, one God, for ever and ever. *Amen.*

II O God, you have given us the Good News of your abounding love in your Son Jesus Christ: So fill our hearts with thankfulness that we may rejoice to proclaim the good tidings we have received; through Jesus Christ our Lord, who lives and reigns with you and the Holy Spirit, one God, for ever and ever. *Amen.*

Psalm	Lessons
34:15–22	Wisdom 2:1a,12–24
	John 7:1–2,10, 25–30

Preface of Lent

Saturday in the Fourth Week of Lent

I Mercifully hear our prayers, O Lord, and spare all those who confess their sins unto thee; that they, whose consciences by sin are accused, by thy merciful pardon may be absolved; through Jesus Christ thy Son our Lord, who liveth and reigneth with thee and the Holy Spirit, one God, for ever and ever. *Amen.*

II Mercifully hear our prayers, O Lord, and spare all those who confess their sins to you; that those whose consciences are accused by sin may by your merciful pardon be absolved; through Jesus Christ your Son our Lord, who lives and reigns with you and the Holy Spirit, one God, for ever and ever. *Amen.*

Psalm	Lessons
7:6–11	Jeremiah 11:18–20
	John 7:37–52

Preface of Lent

Monday in the Fifth Week of Lent

I Be gracious to thy people, we beseech thee, O Lord, that they, repenting day by day of the things that displease thee, may be more and more filled with love of thee and of thy commandments; and, being supported by thy grace in this life, may come to the full enjoyment of eternal life in thine everlasting kingdom; through Jesus Christ our Lord, who liveth and reigneth with thee and the Holy Spirit, one God, for ever and ever. *Amen.*

II Be gracious to your people, we entreat you, O Lord, that they, repenting day by day of the things that displease you, may be more and more filled with love of you and of your commandments; and, being supported by your grace in this life, may come to the full enjoyment of eternal life in your everlasting kingdom; through Jesus Christ our Lord, who lives and reigns with you and the Holy Spirit, one God, for ever and ever. *Amen.*

Psalm	**Lessons**
23	Susanna* 1–9,15–29,34–62
	or verses 41–62
	John 8:1–11
	or John 8:12–20

* In some Bibles, Daniel 13

Another Proper

The following Psalm and Lessons may be used on any weekday of this week (fifth week of Lent), especially in Years B and C.

17:1–8	2 Kings 4:18–21,32–37
	John 11:(1–7)18–44

Preface of Lent

Tuesday in the Fifth Week of Lent

I Almighty God, who through the incarnate Word dost make us to be born anew of an imperishable and eternal seed: Look with compassion, we beseech thee, upon those who are being prepared for Holy Baptism, and grant that they may be built as living stones into a spiritual temple acceptable unto thee; through Jesus Christ our Lord, who liveth and reigneth with thee and the Holy Spirit, one God, for ever and ever. *Amen.*

II Almighty God, through the incarnate Word you have caused us to be born anew of an imperishable and eternal seed: Look with compassion upon those who are being prepared for Holy Baptism, and grant that they may be built as living stones into a spiritual temple acceptable to you; through Jesus Christ our Lord, who lives and reigns with you and the Holy Spirit, one God, for ever and ever. *Amen.*

Psalm	**Lessons**
102:15–22	Numbers 21:4–9
	John 8:21–30

Preface of Lent

Wednesday in the Fifth Week of Lent

I Almighty God our heavenly Father, renew in us the gifts of thy mercy; increase our faith, strengthen our hope, enlighten our understanding, enlarge our charity, and make us ready to serve thee; through Jesus Christ our Lord, who liveth and reigneth with thee and the Holy Spirit, one God, for ever and ever. *Amen.*

II Almighty God our heavenly Father, renew in us the gifts of your mercy; increase our faith, strengthen our hope, enlighten our understanding, widen our charity, and make us ready to serve you; through Jesus Christ our Lord, who lives and reigns with you and the Holy Spirit, one God, for ever and ever. *Amen.*

Psalm	**Lessons**
Canticle 2 or 13	Daniel 3:14–20,24–28
	John 8:31–42

Preface of Lent

Thursday in the Fifth Week of Lent

I O God, who hast called us to be thy children, and hast promised that those who suffer with Christ will be heirs with him of thy glory: Arm us with such trust in him that we may ask no rest from his demands and have no fear in his service; through the same Jesus Christ our Lord, who liveth and reigneth with thee and the Holy Spirit, one God, for ever and ever. *Amen.*

II O God, you have called us to be your children, and have promised that those who suffer with Christ will be heirs with him of your glory: Arm us with such trust in him that we may ask no rest from his demands and have no fear in his service; through Jesus Christ our Lord, who lives and reigns with you and the Holy Spirit, one God, for ever and ever. *Amen.*

Psalm	Lessons
105:4–11	Genesis 17:1–8
	John 8:51–59

Preface of Lent

Friday in the Fifth Week of Lent

I O Lord, who dost, out of the abundance of thy great riches, relieve our necessity: Grant, we beseech thee, that we may accept with joy the salvation thou dost bestow, and by the quality of our lives show forth the same to all the world; through Jesus Christ our Lord, who liveth and reigneth with thee and the Holy Spirit, one God, for ever and ever. *Amen.*

II O Lord, you relieve our necessity out of the abundance of your great riches: Grant that we may accept with joy the salvation you bestow, and manifest it to all the world by the quality of our lives; through Jesus Christ our Lord, who lives and reigns with you and the Holy Spirit, one God, now and for ever. *Amen.*

Psalm	**Lessons**
18:1–7	Jeremiah 20:7–13
	John 10:31–42

Preface of Lent

Saturday in the Fifth Week of Lent

I O Lord, who in thy goodness dost bestow abundant graces on thine elect: Look with favor, we entreat thee, upon those who in these Lenten days are being prepared for Holy Baptism, and grant them the help of thy protection; through Jesus Christ thy Son our Lord, who liveth and reigneth with thee and the Holy Spirit, one God, for ever and ever. *Amen.*

II O Lord, in your goodness you bestow abundant graces on your elect: Look with favor, we entreat you, upon those who in these Lenten days are being prepared for Holy Baptism, and grant them the help of your protection; through Jesus Christ your Son our Lord, who lives and reigns with you and the Holy Spirit, one God, for ever and ever. *Amen.*

Psalm	Lessons
85:1–7	Ezekiel 37:21–28
	John 11:45–53

Preface of Lent

Holy Week

Monday in Holy Week

I   Almighty God, whose most dear Son went not up to joy but first he suffered pain, and entered not into glory before he was crucified: Mercifully grant that we, walking in the way of the cross, may find it none other than the way of life and peace; through the same thy Son Jesus Christ our Lord, who liveth and reigneth with thee and the Holy Spirit, one God, for ever and ever. *Amen.*

II Almighty God, whose most dear Son went not up to joy but first he suffered pain, and entered not into glory before he was crucified: Mercifully grant that we, walking in the way of the cross, may find it none other than the way of life and peace; through Jesus Christ your Son our Lord, who lives and reigns with you and the Holy Spirit, one God, for ever and ever. *Amen.*

Psalm	Lessons
36:5-11	Isaiah 42:1-9
	Hebrews 9:11-15
	John 12:1-11

Preface of Holy Week

Tuesday in Holy Week

I   O God, who by the passion of thy blessed Son didst make an instrument of shameful death to be unto us the means of life: Grant us so to glory in the cross of Christ, that we may gladly suffer shame and loss for the sake of thy Son our Savior Jesus Christ; who liveth and reigneth with thee and the Holy Spirit, one God, for ever and ever. *Amen.*

II   O God, by the passion of your blessed Son you made an instrument of shameful death to be for us the means of life: Grant us so to glory in the cross of Christ, that we may gladly suffer shame and loss for the sake of your Son our Savior Jesus Christ; who lives and reigns with you and the Holy Spirit, one God, for ever and ever. *Amen.*

Psalm	Lessons
71:1-14	Isaiah 49:1-7
	1 Corinthians 1:18-31
	John 12:20-36

Preface of Holy Week

Wednesday in Holy Week

I O Lord God, whose blessed Son our Savior gave his back to the smiters and hid not his face from shame: Grant us grace to take joyfully the sufferings of the present time, in full assurance of the glory that shall be revealed; through the same thy Son Jesus Christ our Lord, who liveth and reigneth with thee and the Holy Spirit, one God, for ever and ever. *Amen.*

II Lord God, whose blessed Son our Savior gave his body to be whipped and his face to be spit upon: Give us grace to accept joyfully the sufferings of the present time, confident of the glory that shall be revealed; through Jesus Christ your Son our Lord, who lives and reigns with you and the Holy Spirit, one God, for ever and ever. *Amen.*

Psalm	Lessons
70	Isaiah 50:4-9a
	Hebrews 12:1-3
	John 13:21-32

Preface of Holy Week

Maundy Thursday

I   Almighty Father, whose dear Son, on the night before he suffered, did institute the Sacrament of his Body and Blood: Mercifully grant that we may thankfully receive the same in remembrance of him who in these holy mysteries giveth us a pledge of life eternal, the same thy Son Jesus Christ our Lord; who now liveth and reigneth with thee and the Holy Spirit ever, one God, world without end. *Amen.*

II   Almighty Father, whose dear Son, on the night before he suffered, instituted the Sacrament of his Body and Blood: Mercifully grant that we may receive it thankfully in remembrance of Jesus Christ our Lord, who in these holy mysteries gives us a pledge of eternal life; and who now lives and reigns with you and the Holy Spirit, one God, for ever and ever. *Amen.*

Psalm	Lessons
116:1,10-17	Exodus 12:1-4,(5-10),11-14
	1 Corinthians 11:23-26
	John 13:1-17,31b-35

Preface of Holy Week

Good Friday

I Almighty God, we beseech thee graciously to behold this thy family, for which our Lord Jesus Christ was contented to be betrayed, and given up into the hands of sinners, and to suffer death upon the cross; who now liveth and reigneth with thee and the Holy Ghost ever, one God, world without end. *Amen.*

II Almighty God, we pray you graciously to behold this your family, for whom our Lord Jesus Christ was willing to be betrayed, and given into the hands of sinners, and to suffer death upon the cross; who now lives and reigns with you and the Holy Spirit, one God, for ever and ever. *Amen.*

Psalm	**Lessons**
22	Isaiah 52:13—53:12
	Hebrews 10:16-25
	or Hebrews 4:14-16; 5:7-9
	John 18:1–19:42

Holy Saturday

I O God, Creator of heaven and earth: Grant that, as the crucified body of thy dear Son was laid in the tomb and rested on this holy Sabbath, so we may await with him the coming of the third day, and rise with him to newness of life; who now liveth and reigneth with thee and the Holy Spirit, one God, for ever and ever. *Amen.*

II O God, Creator of heaven and earth: Grant that, as the crucified body of your dear Son was laid in the tomb and rested on this holy Sabbath, so we may await with him the coming of the third day, and rise with him to newness of life; who now lives and reigns with you and the Holy Spirit, one God, for ever and ever. *Amen.*

Psalm	Lessons
31:1-4,15-16	Job 14:1-14
	or Lamentations 3:1-9,19-24
	1 Peter 4:1-8
	Matthew 27:57-66
	or John 19:38-42

Easter Week

Monday in Easter Week

I Grant, we beseech thee, Almighty God, that we who celebrate with reverence the Paschal feast may be found worthy to attain to everlasting joys; through Jesus Christ our Lord, who liveth and reigneth with thee and the Holy Spirit, one God, now and for ever. *Amen.*

II Grant, we pray, Almighty God, that we who celebrate with awe the Paschal feast may be found worthy to attain to everlasting joys; through Jesus Christ our Lord, who lives and reigns with you and the Holy Spirit, one God, now and for ever. *Amen.*

Psalm	**Lessons**
16:8-11	Acts 2:14,22b-32
or 118:19-24	Matthew 28:9-15

Preface of Easter

Tuesday in Easter Week

I O God, who by the glorious resurrection of thy Son Jesus Christ destroyed death and brought life and immortality to light: Grant that we, who have been raised with him, may abide in his presence and rejoice in the hope of eternal glory; through the same Jesus Christ our Lord, to whom, with thee and the Holy Spirit, be dominion and praise for ever and ever. *Amen.*

II O God, who by the glorious resurrection of your Son Jesus Christ destroyed death and brought life and immortality to light: Grant that we, who have been raised with him, may abide in his presence and rejoice in the hope of eternal glory; through Jesus Christ our Lord, to whom, with you and the Holy Spirit, be dominion and praise for ever and ever. *Amen.*

Psalm	Lessons
33:18-22	Acts 2:36-41
or 118:19-24	John 20:11-18

Preface of Easter

Wednesday in Easter Week

I   O God, whose blessed Son did manifest himself to his disciples in the breaking of bread: Open, we pray thee, the eyes of our faith, that we may behold him in all his redeeming work; through the same thy Son Jesus Christ our Lord, who liveth and reigneth with thee, in the unity of the Holy Spirit, one God, now and for ever. *Amen.*

II   O God, whose blessed Son made himself known to his disciples in the breaking of bread: Open the eyes of our faith, that we may behold him in all his redeeming work; who lives and reigns with you, in the unity of the Holy Spirit, one God, now and for ever. *Amen.*

Psalm	Lessons
105:1-8	Acts 3:1-10
or 118:19-24	Luke 24:13-35

Preface of Easter

Thursday in Easter Week

I Almighty and everlasting God, who in the Paschal mystery hast established the new covenant of reconciliation: Grant that all who have been reborn into the fellowship of Christ's Body may show forth in their lives what they profess by their faith; through the same Jesus Christ our Lord, who liveth and reigneth with thee and the Holy Spirit, one God, for ever and ever. *Amen.*

II Almighty and everlasting God, who in the Paschal mystery established the new covenant of reconciliation: Grant that all who have been reborn into the fellowship of Christ's Body may show forth in their lives what they profess by their faith; through Jesus Christ our Lord, who lives and reigns with you and the Holy Spirit, one God, for ever and ever. *Amen.*

Psalm	Lessons
8	Acts 3:11-26
or 114	Luke 24:36b-48
or 118:19-24	

Preface of Easter

Friday in Easter Week

I   Almighty Father, who hast given thine only Son to die for our sins and to rise again for our justification: Grant us so to put away the leaven of malice and wickedness, that we may always serve thee in pureness of living and truth; through the same thy Son Jesus Christ our Lord, who liveth and reigneth with thee and the Holy Spirit, one God, now and for ever. *Amen.*

II Almighty Father, who gave your only Son to die for our sins and to rise for our justification: Give us grace so to put away the leaven of malice and wickedness, that we may always serve you in pureness of living and truth; through Jesus Christ your Son our Lord, who lives and reigns with you and the Holy Spirit, one God, now and for ever. *Amen.*

Psalm	**Lessons**
116:1-8	Acts 4:1-12
or 118:19-24	John 21:1-14

Preface of Easter

Saturday in Easter Week

I We thank thee, heavenly Father, for that thou hast delivered us from the dominion of sin and death and hast brought us into the kingdom of thy Son; and we pray thee that, as by his death he hath recalled us to life, so by his love he may raise us to joys eternal; who liveth and reigneth with thee, in the unity of the Holy Spirit, one God, now and for ever. *Amen.*

II We thank you, heavenly Father, that you have delivered us from the dominion of sin and death and brought us into the kingdom of your Son; and we pray that, as by his death he has recalled us to life, so by his love he may raise us to eternal joys; who lives and reigns with you, in the unity of the Holy Spirit, one God, now and for ever. *Amen.*

Psalm

118:14-18
or 118:19-24

Lessons

Acts 4:13-21
Mark 16:9-15,20

Preface of Easter

Weekdays of Easter Season

Concerning the Proper

Proper Lessons and Psalms are provided for the weekdays of Easter Season. The First Lessons consist of a semi-continuous reading of the Acts of the Apostles (which is an ancient tradition in this season), the earlier portions of which are appointed in the Prayer Book Lectionary for the weekdays of Easter Week. The Readings from the Gospel according to John are chosen for their appropriateness to the season, and complement the Readings from this Gospel assigned to the season of Lent.

Any of the Readings may be lengthened at discretion. The selections from the Psalter may be lengthened or shortened.

Where there is not a daily celebration of the Eucharist, the Proper appointed for any weekday may be used on any other weekday in the same week.

Since the triumphs of the saints are a continuation and manifestation of the Paschal victory of Christ, the celebration of saints' days is particularly appropriate during this season. On such days, therefore, the Collect, Lessons, Psalm, and Preface are ordinarily those of the saint. Where there is a daily celebration, however, the weekday Lessons and Psalm may be substituted.

A corpus of Collects is provided for use as the Collect of the Day on weekdays which are not saints' days. These Collects are also appropriate for use at the conclusion of the Prayers of the People during this season, including the Sundays.

The Collects which follow are particularly appropriate for use at the times indicated.
The Lessons and Psalms for this season are on pages 70-75.

From Monday after 2 Easter until 4 Easter

1

I O God, who hast united divers peoples in the confession of thy Name: Grant, we pray thee, that all who have been born again in the font of Baptism may also be united in faith and love; through Jesus Christ our Lord, who liveth and reigneth with thee and the Holy Spirit, one God, for ever and ever. *Amen.*

II O God, you have united diverse peoples in the confession of your Name: Grant that all who have been born again in the font of Baptism may also be united in faith and love; through Jesus Christ our Lord, who lives and reigns with you and the Holy Spirit, one God, for ever and ever. *Amen.*

2

I O God, who by the waters of Baptism hast renewed those who believe in thee: Come to the help of those who have been reborn in Christ, that they may overcome the wiles of the devil, and continue faithful to the gifts of grace that they have received from thee; through Jesus Christ our Lord, who liveth and reigneth with thee and the Holy Spirit, one God, for ever and ever. *Amen.*

II   O God, by the waters of Baptism you have renewed those who believe in you: Come to the help of those who have been reborn in Christ, that they may overcome the wiles of the devil, and continue faithful to the gifts of grace they have received from you; through Jesus Christ our Lord, who lives and reigns with you and the Holy Spirit, one God, for ever and ever. *Amen.*

3

I   Grant, O Lord, we beseech thee, that we may so live in the Paschal mystery that the joy of these fifty days may continually strengthen us, and assure us of our salvation; through Jesus Christ thy Son our Lord, who liveth and reigneth with thee and the Holy Spirit, one God, for ever and ever. *Amen.*

II   Grant, O Lord, that we may so live in the Paschal mystery that the joy of these fifty days may continually strengthen us, and assure us of our salvation; through Jesus Christ your Son our Lord, who lives and reigns with you and the Holy Spirit, one God, for ever and ever. *Amen.*

4

I   O Lord, who hast saved us through the Paschal mystery of Christ: Continue to support thy people with heavenly gifts, that we may attain unto true liberty, and enjoy the happiness of heaven which we have begun to taste on earth; through Jesus Christ our Lord, who liveth and reigneth with thee and the Holy Spirit, one God, for ever and ever. *Amen.*

II O Lord, you have saved us through the Paschal mystery of Christ: Continue to support your people with heavenly gifts, that we may attain true liberty, and enjoy the happiness of heaven which we have begun to taste on earth; through Jesus Christ our Lord, who lives and reigns with you and the Holy Spirit, one God, for ever and ever. *Amen.*

5

I O Lord, who art the life of the faithful, the glory of the saints, and the delight of those who trust in thee: Hear our supplications, and quench, we pray thee, the thirst of those who long for thy promises; through Jesus Christ our Lord, who liveth and reigneth with thee and Holy Spirit, one God, for ever and ever. *Amen.*

II O Lord, the life of the faithful, the glory of the saints, and the delight of those who trust in you: Hear our supplications, and quench, we pray, the thirst of those who long for your promises; through Jesus Christ our Lord, who lives and reigns with you and the Holy Spirit, one God, for ever and ever. *Amen.*

6

I O God, who by the abundance of thy grace dost unfailingly increase the number of thy children: Look with favor upon those whom thou hast chosen to be members of thy Church, that, having been born again in Baptism, they may be granted a glorious resurrection; through Jesus Christ thy Son our Lord, who liveth and reigneth with thee and the Holy Spirit, one God, now and for ever. *Amen.*

II O God, by the abundance of your grace you unfailingly increase the number of your children: Look with favor upon those whom you have chosen to be members of your Church, that, having been born again in Baptism, they may be granted a glorious resurrection; through Jesus Christ your Son our Lord, who lives and reigns with you and the Holy Spirit, one God, now and for ever. *Amen.*

7

I Let thy people, O Lord, rejoice for ever that they have been renewed in spirit; and let the joy of our adoption as thy sons and daughters strengthen the hope of our glorious resurrection in Jesus Christ our Lord; who liveth and reigneth with thee and the Holy Spirit, one God, for ever and ever. *Amen.*

II Let your people, O Lord, rejoice for ever that they have been renewed in spirit; and let the joy of our adoption as your sons and daughters strengthen the hope of our glorious resurrection in Jesus Christ our Lord; who lives and reigns with you and the Holy Spirit, one God, for ever and ever. *Amen.*

From Monday after 4 Easter until Ascension Day

8

I   Almighty and everlasting God, who hast given unto thy Church the great joy of the resurrection of Jesus Christ: Give us also the greater joy of the kingdom of thine elect, when the flock of thy Son will share in the final victory of its Shepherd, Jesus Christ our Lord; who liveth and reigneth with thee and the Holy Spirit, one God, now and for ever. *Amen.*

II   Almighty and everlasting God, you have given your Church the great joy of the resurrection of Jesus Christ: Give us also the greater joy of the kingdom of your elect, when the flock of your Son will share in the final victory of its Shepherd, Jesus Christ our Lord; who lives and reigns with you and the Holy Spirit, one God, now and for ever. *Amen.*

9

I   Almighty God, who showest to them that are in error the light of thy truth, to the intent that they may return into the way of righteousness: Grant unto all those who are admitted into the fellowship of Christ's religion that they may avoid those things that are contrary to their profession, and follow all such things as are agreeable to the same; through Jesus Christ our Lord, who liveth and reigneth with thee and the Holy Spirit, one God, for ever and ever. *Amen.*

II Almighty God, you show the light of your truth to those who are in error, to the intent that they may return to the way of righteousness: Grant to those who are admitted into the fellowship of Christ's religion that they may avoid those things that are contrary to their profession, and follow all such things as are agreeable to it; through Jesus Christ our Lord, who lives and reigns with you and the Holy Spirit, one God, for ever and ever. *Amen.*

10

I God of infinite mercy, who dost renew the faith of thy people by the yearly celebration of these fifty days: Stir up in us, we beseech thee, the gifts of thy grace, that we may more deeply know that Baptism hath cleansed us, the Spirit hath quickened us, and the Blood of Christ hath redeemed us; through the same Jesus Christ our Lord, who liveth and reigneth with thee and the same Holy Spirit, one God, for ever and ever. *Amen.*

II God of infinite mercy, you renew the faith of your people by the yearly celebration of these fifty days: Stir up in us the gifts of your grace, that we may know more deeply that Baptism has cleansed us, the Spirit has quickened us, and the Blood of Christ has redeemed us; through Jesus Christ our Lord, who lives and reigns with you and the Holy Spirit, one God, for ever and ever. *Amen.*

11

I Lord God Almighty, who for no merit on our part hast brought us out of death into life, out of sorrow into joy: Put no end to thy gifts, fulfill thy marvelous acts in us, and grant unto us who have been justified by faith the strength to persevere in that faith; through Jesus Christ our Lord, who liveth and reigneth with thee and the Holy Spirit, one God, for ever and ever. *Amen.*

II Lord God Almighty, for no merit on our part you have brought us out of death into life, out of sorrow into joy: Put no end to your gifts, fulfill your marvelous acts in us, and grant to us who have been justified by faith the strength to persevere in that faith; through Jesus Christ our Lord, who lives and reigns with you and the Holy Spirit, one God, for ever and ever. *Amen.*

12

I O God, who dost continually increase thy Church by the birth of new sons and daughters in Baptism: Grant that they may be obedient all the days of their life to the rule of faith which they did receive in that Sacrament; through Jesus Christ thy Son our Lord, who liveth and reigneth with thee and the Holy Spirit, one God, now and for ever. *Amen.*

II O God, you continually increase your Church by the birth of new sons and daughters in Baptism: Grant that they may be obedient all the days of their life to the rule of faith which they received in that Sacrament; through Jesus Christ your Son our Lord, who lives and reigns with you and the Holy Spirit, one God, now and for ever. *Amen.*

13

I   Grant, Almighty God, we beseech thee, that the commemoration of our Lord's death and resurrection may continually transform our lives and be manifest in our deeds; through Jesus Christ our Lord, who liveth and reigneth with thee and the Holy Spirit, one God, for ever and ever. *Amen.*

II Grant, Almighty God, that the commemoration of our Lord's death and resurrection may continually transform our lives and be manifested in our deeds; through Jesus Christ our Lord, who lives and reigns with you and the Holy Spirit, one God, for ever and ever. *Amen.*

14

I   Hear our prayers, O Lord, and, as we confess that Christ, the Savior of the world, doth live with thee in glory, grant that, as he himself hath promised, we may perceive him present among us also, to the end of the ages; who liveth and reigneth with thee and the Holy Spirit, one God, for ever and ever. *Amen.*

II Hear our prayers, O Lord, and, as we confess that Christ, the Savior of the world, lives with you in glory, grant that, as he himself has promised, we may perceive him present among us also, to the end of the ages; who lives and reigns with you and the Holy Spirit, one God, for ever and ever. *Amen.*

15

I O Lord, who hast given unto us the grace to know the resurrection of thy Son: Grant that the Holy Spirit, by his love, may raise us to newness of life; through Jesus Christ our Lord, who liveth and reigneth with thee and the same Spirit, one God, for ever and ever. *Amen.*

II O Lord, you have given us the grace to know the resurrection of your Son: Grant that the Holy Spirit, by his love, may raise us to newness of life; through Jesus Christ our Lord, who lives and reigns with you and the Holy Spirit, one God, for ever and ever. *Amen.*

16

I O Lord, who openest the portals of thy kingdom to those who have been reborn by water and the Spirit: Increase the grace which thou hast given to thy children, that those whom thou hast cleansed from sin may attain to all thy promises; through Jesus Christ our Lord, who liveth and reigneth with thee and the Holy Spirit, one God, now and for ever. *Amen.*

II O Lord, you open the portals of your kingdom to those who have been reborn by water and the Spirit: Increase the grace you have given to your children, that those whom you have cleansed from sin may attain to all your promises; through Jesus Christ our Lord, who lives and reigns with you and the Holy Spirit, one God, for ever and ever. *Amen.*

From Friday after Ascension Day until Pentecost

17

I O God, who by the resurrection of thy Son hast given unto us a new birth into eternal life: Lift our hearts, we beseech thee, to our Savior, who sitteth at thy right hand, that, when he shall come again, we who have been reborn in Baptism may be clothed in a glorious immortality; through Jesus Christ our Lord, who liveth and reigneth with thee and the Holy Spirit, one God, for ever and ever. *Amen.*

II O God, by the resurrection of your Son you have given us a new birth into eternal life: Lift our hearts to our Savior, who is seated at your right hand, so that, when he comes again, we who have been reborn in Baptism may be clothed in a glorious immortality; through Jesus Christ our Lord, who lives and reigns with you and the Holy Spirit, one God, for ever and ever. *Amen.*

18

I O God, who by the glorification of Jesus Christ and the coming of the Holy Spirit hast opened for us the gates of thy kingdom: Grant that we, who have received such great gifts, may dedicate ourselves more diligently to thy service, and live more fully the riches of our faith; through Jesus Christ our Lord, who liveth and reigneth with thee and the Holy Spirit, one God, for ever and ever. *Amen.*

II O God, by the glorification of Jesus Christ and the coming of the Holy Spirit you have opened for us the gates of your kingdom: Grant that we, who have received such great gifts, may dedicate ourselves more diligently to your service, and live more fully the riches of our faith; through

Jesus Christ our Lord, who lives and reigns with you and the Holy Spirit, one God, for ever and ever. *Amen.*

19

I   O Lord, whose Son, after he had ascended into heaven, did send down upon the Apostles the Holy Spirit, as he had promised, that they might comprehend the mysteries of the kingdom: Distribute among us also, we pray thee, the gifts of that selfsame Spirit; through Jesus Christ our Lord, who liveth and reigneth with thee and the same Holy Spirit, one God, for ever and ever. *Amen.*

II   O Lord, when your Son ascended into heaven he sent down upon the Apostles the Holy Spirit, as he had promised, that they might comprehend the mysteries of the kingdom: Distribute among us also, we pray, the gifts of the selfsame Spirit; through Jesus Christ our Lord, who lives and reigns with you and the Holy Spirit, one God, for ever and ever. *Amen.*

20

I   O loving Father, grant, we pray thee, that thy Church, being gathered by thy Holy Spirit, may be dedicated more fully to thy service, and live united in love, according to thy will; through Jesus Christ our Lord, who liveth and reigneth with thee and the same Spirit, one God, for ever and ever. *Amen.*

II   O loving Father, grant that your Church, being gathered by your Holy Spirit, may be dedicated more fully to your service, and live united in love, according to your will; through Jesus Christ our Lord, who lives and reigns with you and the Holy Spirit, one God, for ever and ever. *Amen.*

The Second Week of Easter

	Psalms	Lessons
Monday	2:1–9*	Acts 4:23–31
	or 146:4–9	John 3:1–8
Tuesday	93	Acts 4:32–37
		John 3:7–15
Wednesday	34:1–8	Acts 5:12–26
		John 3:16–21
Thursday	34:15–22	Acts 5:27–33
		John 3:31–36
Friday	27:1–9	Acts 5:34–42
		John 6:1–15
Saturday	33:1–5,18–22	Acts 6:1–7
		John 6:16–21

Preface of Easter

* *Appointed also at Morning Prayer on this Day.*

The Third Week of Easter

	Psalms	Lessons
Monday	27:10–18	Acts 6:8–15
		John 6:22–29
Tuesday	31:1–5	Acts 7:51–8:1a
		John 6:30–35
Wednesday	66:1–8	Acts 8:1b–8
		John 6:35–40
Thursday	66:14–18 (Years A & B)	Acts 8:26–40 (Years A & B)
	65:1–5 (Year C)	Acts 8:9–25 (Year C)
		John 6:44–51
Friday	117	Acts 9:1–20 (Years A & B)
		Acts 9:10–20,26–31 (Year C)
		John 6:52–59
Saturday	116:10–17	Acts 9:31–42 (Years A & B)
		Acts 10:1–5,25–31,34–35,44–48 (Year C)
		John 6:60–69

Preface of Easter

The Fourth Week of Easter

	Psalms	Lessons
Monday	96:1–9	Acts 11:1–18
		John 10:11–18 (Year A)
		John 10:1–10 (Years B & C)
Tuesday	87	Acts 11:19–26
		John 10:22–30
Wednesday	67	Acts 12:24–13:5a
		John 12:44–50
Thursday	89:20–29	Acts 13:13–25
		John 13:16–20
Friday	2:6–13	Acts 13:26–33
		John 14:1–6
Saturday	98:1–6 (Years A & B)	Acts 13:44–52 (Years A & B)
	16:5–11 (Year C)	Acts 13:32–43 (Year C)
		John 14:7–14

Preface of Easter

The Fifth Week of Easter

	Psalms	Lessons
Monday	115:1–13	Acts 14:5–18
		John 14:21–26
Tuesday	145:9–14	Acts 14:19–28
		John 14:27–31a
Wednesday	122	Acts 15:1–6
		John 15:1–8
Thursday	96:1–10	Acts 15:7–21
		John 15:9–11
Friday	57:6–11	Acts 15:22–31
		John 15:12–17
Saturday	100	Acts 16:1–10
		John 15:18–21

Preface of Easter

The Sixth Week of Easter

	Psalms	Lessons
Monday	149	Acts 16:11–15
		John 15:26–16:4a
Tuesday	138	Acts 16:16–34
		John 16:5–11
Wednesday	148:1–2,11–14	Acts 17:15,22–18:1
		John 16:12–15

Preface of Easter

Friday	98:1–4	Acts 18:1–8
		John 16:20–23a
Saturday	47	Acts 18:23–28
	or 93	John 16:23b–28

Preface of the Ascension

The Seventh Week of Easter

	Psalms	Lessons
Monday	68:1–8	Acts 19:1–8
		John 16:28–33
Tuesday	68:9–10,17–20	Acts 20:17–27
		John 17:1–11a
Wednesday	68:28–36	Acts 20:28–38
		John 17:11b–19
Thursday	16:5–11	Acts 22:30;23:6–11
		John 17:20–26
Friday	103:1–2,19–22	Acts 25:13–21
		John 21:15–19
Saturday	11:4–8	Acts 28:16–20,30–31
		John 21:20–25

Preface of the Ascension

Ordinary Time (the Seasons after Epiphany and Pentecost): A Two-Year Weekday Eucharistic Lectionary

(Adapted from The Book of Alternative Services *of the Anglican Church of Canada)*

Concerning the Lectionary

This Weekday Lectionary offers a two-year cycle of sequential readings and is intended for use on the weekdays following the First Sunday after the Epiphany and the Day of Pentecost.

The Lectionary is arranged in a two-year cycle. The Year-1 cycle is used in odd-numbered years, and the Year-2 cycle is used in even-numbered years. The numbered Propers for the weeks following the Day of Pentecost, and for some weeks in Epiphany season, correspond to the numbering and dating system used in the Book of Common Prayer.

Two daily readings are provided. All references to readings are based on the New Revised Standard Version of the Bible. Versification varies among translations; if another translation is being used, the NRSV should be checked.

All references to psalms are based on the Psalter of the Book of Common Prayer. Verse selections are suggested for many psalms, but selections may be lengthened or shortened as appropriate.

The Collect of the previous Sunday may be used on ordinary weekdays.

Key: 1—Year 1 2—Year 2 C—Canticle from the Book of Common Prayer

Week of the Baptism of Our Lord—1 Epiphany

Mon
1 Heb. 1:1–6   Ps. 97   Mark 1:14–20
2 1 Sam. 1:1–8   Ps. 116:10–17   Mark 1:14–20

Tue
1 Heb. 2:5–12   Ps. 8   Mark 1:21–28
2 1 Sam. 1:9–20   C15 *or* Ps. 123   Mark 1:21–28

Wed
1 Heb. 2:14–18   Ps. 105:1–15   Mark 1:29–39
2 1 Sam. 3:1–20   Ps. 40:1–10   Mark 1:29–39

Thu
1 Heb. 3:1–14   Ps. 95:6–11   Mark 1:40–45
2 1 Sam. 4:1c–11   Ps. 44:7–14,23–26   Mark 1:40–45

Fri
1 Heb. 4:1–5,11   Ps. 78:3–8   Mark 2:1–12
2 1 Sam. 8:4–7,10–22a Ps. 89:15–18   Mark 2:1–12

Sat
1 Heb. 4:12–16   Ps. 19:7–14   Mark 2:13–17
2 1 Sam. 9:1–4,15–19; Ps. 21:1–7   Mark 2:13–17
  10:1ab (not c)

Week of 2 Epiphany

Mon

1 Heb. 5:1–10	Ps. 110	Mark 2:18–22
2 1 Sam. 15:16–23	Ps. 50:7–15,24	Mark 2:18–22

Tue

1 Heb. 6:10–20	Ps. 111	Mark 2:23–28
2 1 Sam. 16:1–13	Ps. 89:19–27	Mark 2:23–28

Wed

1 Heb. 7:1–3,15–17	Ps. 110	Mark 3:1–6
2 1 Sam. 17:32–51	Ps. 144:1–10	Mark 3:1–6

Thu

1 Heb. 7:23–8:7	Ps. 40:8–12,17–19	Mark 3:7–12
2 1 Sam. 18:6–9; 19:1–8	Ps. 56	Mark 3:7–12

Fri

1 Heb. 8:6–13	Ps. 85:7–13	Mark 3:13–19
2 1 Sam. 24:2–20	Ps. 57	Mark 3:13–19

Sat

1 Heb. 9:2–3,11–14	Ps. 47	John 8:51–59
2 2 Sam. 1:1–4, 11–12, 19–27	Ps. 80:1–7	John 8:51–59

Week of 3 Epiphany

Mon
1 Heb. 9:15,24–28   Ps. 98   Mark 3:19b–30
2 2 Sam. 5:1–7,10   Ps. 89:19–28   Mark 3:19b–30

Tue
1 Heb. 10:1–10   Ps. 40:1–11   Mark 3:31–35
2 2 Sam. 6:12b–19   Ps. 24:7–10   Mark 3:31–35

Wed
1 Heb. 10:11–18   Ps. 110:1–4   Mark 4:1–20
2 2 Sam. 7:4–17   Ps. 89:1–4   Mark 4:1–20

Thu
1 Heb. 10:19–25   Ps. 24:1–6   Mark 4:21–25
2 2 Sam. 7:18–19, 24–29   Ps. 132:1–5,11–15   Mark 4:21–25

Fri
1 Heb. 10:32–39   Ps. 37:1–7,24–25, 41–42   Mark 4:26–34
2 2 Sam. 11:1–17   Ps. 51:1–10   Mark 4:26–34

Sat
1 Heb. 11:1–2,8–19   C16 *or* Ps. 89:19–29   Mark 4:35–41
2 2 Sam. 12:1–25   Ps. 51:11–18   Mark 4:35–41

Week of 4 Epiphany

Mon

1 Heb. 11:32–40	Ps. 31:19–24	Mark 5:1–20
2 2 Sam. 15:13–14,30; 16:5–14	Ps. 3	Mark 5:1–20

Tue

1 Heb. 12:1–4	Ps. 22:22–30	Mark 5:21–43
2 2 Sam. 18:9–14, 24–19:3	Ps. 86:1–6	Mark 5:21–43

Wed

1 Heb. 12:4–7,11–15	Ps. 103:1–2,13–18	Mark 6:1–6
2 2 Sam. 24:2,9–17	Ps. 32:1–8	Mark 6:1–6

Thu

1 Heb. 12:18–24	Ps. 48:1–3,7–9	Mark 6:7–13
2 1 Kings 2:1–4, 10–12	Ps. 132:10–19	Mark 6:7–13

Fri

1 Heb. 13:1–8	Ps. 27:1–13	Mark 6:14–29
2 Ecclus. 47:2–11	Ps. 18:31–33,46–50	Mark 6:14–29

Sat

1 Heb. 13:9–17,20–21	Ps. 23	Mark 6:30–34
2 1 Kings 3:3–14	Ps. 119:9–16	Mark 6:30–34

Week of 5 Epiphany

Mon

1 Gen. 1:1–19	Ps. 104:1–12,25	Mark 6:53–56
2 1 Kings 8:1–7,9–13	Ps. 132:6–10	Mark 6:53–56

Tue

1 Gen. 1:20–2:4a	Ps. 8	Mark 7:1–13
2 1 Kings 8:22–23,27–30	Ps. 84	Mark 7:1–13

Wed

1 Gen. 2:4b–9,15–17	Ps. 104:25,28–31	Mark 7:14–23
2 1 Kings 10:1–10	Ps. 37:1–7,32–33, 41–42	Mark 7:14–23

Thu

1 Gen. 2:18–25	Ps. 128	Mark 7:24–30
2 1 Kings 11:4–13	Ps. 132:11–19	Mark 7:24–30

Fri

1 Gen. 3:1–8	Ps. 32:1–8	Mark 7:31–37
2 1 Kings 11:29–32;12:19	Ps. 81:8–16	Mark 7:31–37

Sat

1 Gen. 3:9–24	Ps. 90:1–12	Mark 8:1–10
2 1 Kings 12:26–33; 13:33–34	Ps. 106:19–22	Mark 8:1–10

Week of 6 Epiphany (*or* Proper 1)

Mon
1 Gen. 4:1–15,25	Ps. 50:7–24	Mark 8:11–13
2 James 1:1–11	Ps. 119:65–72	Mark 8:11–13

Tue
1 Gen. 6:5–8;7:1–5,10	Ps. 29	Mark 8:14–21
2 James 1:12–18	Ps. 94:12–19	Mark 8:14–21

Wed
1 Gen. 8:6–13,20–22	Ps. 116:10–17	Mark 8:22–26
2 James 1:19–27	Ps. 15	Mark 8:22–26

Thu
1 Gen. 9:1–13	Ps. 102:15–22	Mark 8:27–33
2 James 2:1–9	Ps. 72:1–4,13–14	Mark 8:27–33

Fri
1 Gen. 11:1–9	Ps. 33:6–18	Mark 8:34–9:1
2 James 2:14–26	Ps. 112	Mark 8:34–9:1

Sat
1 Heb. 11:1–7	Ps. 145:1–4,10–13	Mark 9:2–13
2 James 3:1–10	Ps. 12:1–7	Mark 9:2–13

Week of 7 Epiphany (*or* Proper 2)

Mon
1 Ecclus. 1:1–10	Ps. 93	Mark 9:14–29
2 James 3:13–18	Ps. 19:7–14	Mark 9:14–29

Tue
1 Ecclus. 2:1–11	Ps. 112	Mark 9:30–37
2 James 4:1–10	Ps. 51:11–18	Mark 9:30–37

Wed
1 Ecclus. 4:11–19	Ps. 119:161–168	Mark 9:38–41
2 James 4:13–17	Ps. 49:1–9,16–20	Mark 9:38–41

Thu
1 Ecclus. 5:1–8	Ps. 1	Mark 9:42–50
2 James 5:1–6	Ps. 49:12–19	Mark 9:42–50

Fri
1 Ecclus. 6:5–17	Ps. 119:17–24	Mark 10:1–12
2 James 5:9–12	Ps. 103:1–4,8–13	Mark 10:1–12

Sat
1 Ecclus. 17:1–15	Ps. 103:1–4,13–18	Mark 10:13–16
2 James 5:13–20	Ps. 34:1–8	Mark 10:13–16

Week of 8 Epiphany (*or* Proper 3)

Mon

1 Ecclus. 17:24–29	Ps. 32:1–8	Mark 10:17–27
2 1 Pet. 1:3–9	Ps. 111	Mark 10:17–27

Tue

1 Ecclus. 35:1–12	Ps. 50:7–15	Mark 10:28–31
2 1 Pet. 1:10–16	Ps. 98	Mark 10:28–31

Wed

1 Ecclus. 36:1–2,5–6, 13–17	Ps. 79:8–13	Mark 10:32–45
2 1 Pet. 1:18–2:1	Ps. 147:13–21	Mark 10:32–45

Thu

1 Ecclus. 42:15–25	Ps. 33:1–9	Mark 10:46–52
2 1 Pet. 2:2–5,9–12	Ps. 100	Mark 10:46–52

Fri

1 Ecclus. 44:1–13	Ps. 149:1–5	Mark 11:11–26
2 1 Pet. 4:7–13	Ps. 96:7–13	Mark 11:11–26

Sat

1 Ecclus. 51:11b–22	Ps. 19:7–14	Mark 11:27–33
2 Jude 1:17–25	Ps. 63:1–8	Mark 11:27–33

Week of Last Epiphany (*or* **Proper 4**)

Note: The lessons for Wednesday through Saturday of this week are used only for Proper 4. When observing the week of Last Epiphany, the Lenten propers are used beginning on Ash Wednesday.

Mon

1 Tobit 1:1–2;2:1–8	Ps. 112:1–6	Mark 12:1–12
2 2 Pet. 1:2–7	Ps. 91	Mark 12:1–12

Tue

1 Tobit 2:9–14	Ps. 112:1–2,7–9	Mark 12:13–17
2 2 Pet. 3:11–18	Ps. 90:1–6,13–17	Mark 12:13–17

Wed

1 Tobit 3:1–11,16–17	Ps. 25:1–8	Mark 12:18–27
2 2 Tim. 1:1–12	Ps. 123	Mark 12:18–27

Thu

1 Tobit 6:9–11;7:1–15	Ps. 128	Mark 12:28–34
2 2 Tim. 2:8–15	Ps. 25:1–12	Mark 12:28–34

Fri

1 Tobit 11:5–15	Ps. 146	Mark 12:35–37
2 2 Tim. 3:10–17	Ps. 119:161–168	Mark 12:35–37

Sat

1 Tobit 12:1,5–15,20	Ps. 65:1–4	Mark 12:38–44
2 2 Tim. 4:1–8	Ps. 71:8–17	Mark 12:38–44

The Season after Pentecost

Week of Proper 5

Mon
1 2 Cor. 1:1–7   Ps. 34:1–8   Matt. 5:1–12
2 1 Kings 17:1–6   Ps. 121   Matt. 5:1–12

Tue
1 2 Cor. 1:18–22   Ps. 119:129–136   Matt. 5:13–16
2 1 Kings 17:7–16   Ps. 4   Matt. 5:13–16

Wed
1 2 Cor. 3:4–11   Ps. 99   Matt. 5:17–19
2 1 Kings 18:20–39   Ps. 16:1,6–11   Matt. 5:17–19

Thu
1 2 Cor. 3:12–4:6   Ps. 85:7–13   Matt. 5:20–26
2 1 Kings 18:41–46   Ps. 65:1,8–14   Matt. 5:20–26

Fri
1 2 Cor. 4:7–15   Ps. 116:9–17   Matt. 5:27–32
2 1 Kings 19:9–16   Ps. 27:10–18   Matt. 5:27–32

Sat
1 2 Cor. 5:14–21   Ps. 103:1–12   Matt. 5:33–37
2 1 Kings 19:19–21   Ps. 16:1–7   Matt. 5:33–37

Week of Proper 6

Mon

1 2 Cor. 6:1–10   Ps. 98   Matt. 5:38–42
2 1 Kings 21:1–16   Ps. 5:1–6   Matt. 5:38–42

Tue

1 2 Cor. 8:1–9   Ps. 146   Matt. 5:43–48
2 1 Kings 21:17–29   Ps. 51:1–11   Matt. 5:43–48

Wed

1 2 Cor. 9:6–11   Ps. 112:1–9   Matt. 6:1–6,16–18
2 2 Kings 2:1,6–14   Ps. 31:19–24   Matt. 6:1–6,16–18

Thu

1 2 Cor. 11:1–11   Ps. 111   Matt. 6:7–15
2 Ecclus. 48:1–14   Ps. 97   Matt. 6:7–15

Fri

1 2 Cor. 11:18,21b–30   Ps. 34:1–6   Matt. 6:19–23
2 2 Kings 11:1–4,9–20   Ps. 132:11–19   Matt. 6:19–23

Sat

1 2 Cor. 12:1–10   Ps. 34:7–14   Matt. 6:24–34
2 2 Chron. 24:17–25   Ps. 89:19–33   Matt. 6:24–34

Week of Proper 7

Mon
1 Gen. 12:1–9   Ps. 33:12–22   Matt. 7:1–5
2 2 Kings 17:5–8,13–18   Ps. 60   Matt. 7:1–5

Tue
1 Gen. 13:2,5–18   Ps. 15   Matt. 7:6,12–14
2 2 Kings 19:9–21,31–36   Ps. 48   Matt. 7:6,12–14

Wed
1 Gen. 15:1–12,17–18   Ps. 47   Matt. 7:15–20
2 2 Kings 22:8–13;23:1–3   Ps. 119:33–40   Matt. 7:15–20

Thu
1 Gen. 16:1–12,15–16   Ps. 106:1–5   Matt. 7:21–29
2 2 Kings 24:8–17   Ps. 79   Matt. 7:21–29

Fri
1 Gen. 17:1,9–10,15–22   Ps. 128   Matt. 8:1–4
2 2 Kings 25:1–12   Ps. 137:1–6   Matt. 8:1–4

Sat
1 Gen. 18:1–15   C15 *or* Ps. 123   Matt. 8:5–17
2 Lam. 2:2,10–14,18–19   Ps. 74:1–8,17–20   Matt. 8:5–17

Week of Proper 8

Mon
1 Gen. 18:16–33   Ps. 103:1–10   Matt. 8:18–22
2 Amos 2:6–10,13–16   Ps. 50:14–24   Matt. 8:18–22

Tue
1 Gen. 19:15–29   Ps. 26   Matt. 8:23–27
2 Amos 3:1–8;4:11–12   Ps. 5   Matt. 8:23–27

Wed
1 Gen. 21:5,8–20   Ps. 34:1–8   Matt. 8:28–34
2 Amos 5:14–15,21–24   Ps. 50:7–15   Matt. 8:28–34

Thu
1 Gen. 22:1–14   Ps. 116:1–8   Matt. 9:1–8
2 Amos 7:10–17   Ps. 19:7–10   Matt. 9:1–8

Fri
1 Gen. 23:1–4,19 ;   Ps. 78:1–8   Matt. 9:9–13
  24:1–8,62–67
2 Amos 8:4–6,9–12   Ps. 119:1–8   Matt. 9:9–13

Sat
1 Gen. 27:1–9,15–29   Ps. 135:1–6   Matt. 9:14–17
2 Amos 9:11–15   Ps. 85:7–13   Matt. 9:14–17

Week of Proper 9

Mon

1 Gen. 28:10–22	Ps. 91:1–6,14–16	Matt. 9:18–26
2 Hosea 2:16–23	Ps. 138	Matt. 9:18–26

Tue

1 Gen. 32:22–32	Ps. 17:1–8	Matt. 9:32–38
2 Hosea 8:4–7,11–13	Ps. 115:1–10	Matt. 9:32–38

Wed

1 Gen. 41:55–57; 42:5–7a,17–24a	Ps. 33:1–4,18–22	Matt. 10:1–7
2 Hosea 10:1–3,7–8,12	Ps. 105:1–7	Matt. 10:1–7

Thu

1 Gen. 44:18–45:5	Ps. 105:7–21	Matt. 10:7–15
2 Hosea 11:1–9	Ps. 80:1–7	Matt. 10:7–15

Fri

1 Gen. 46:1–7,28–30	Ps. 37:3–4,19–20, 28–29,41–42	Matt. 10:16–23
2 Hosea 14:1–9	Ps. 51:1–12	Matt. 10:16–23

Sat

1 Gen. 49:29–33	Ps. 105:1–7	Matt. 10:24–33
2 Isa. 6:1–8	Ps. 93	Matt. 10:24–33

Week of Proper 10

Mon
1 Exod. 1:8–14,22   Ps. 124   Matt. 10:34–11:1
2 Isa. 1:10–17   Ps. 50:7–15   Matt. 10:34–11:1

Tue
1 Exod. 2:1–15   Ps. 69:1–2,31–38 Matt. 11:20–24
2 Isa. 7:1–9   Ps. 48   Matt. 11:20–24

Wed
1 Exod. 3:1–12   Ps. 103:1–7   Matt. 11:25–27
2 Isa. 10:5–7,13–16 Ps. 94:5–15   Matt. 11:25–27

Thu
1 Exod. 3:13–20   Ps. 105:1–15   Matt. 11:28–30
2 Isa. 26:7–9,12,16–19 Ps. 102:12–22 Matt. 11:28–30

Fri
1 Exod. 11:10–12:14 Ps. 116:10–17   Matt. 12:1–8
2 Isa. 38:1–6,21   Ps. 6   Matt. 12:1–8

Sat
1 Exod. 12:37–42   Ps. 136:1–3,10–15 Matt. 12:14–21
2 Micah 2:1–5   Ps. 10:1–9,18–19 Matt. 12:14–21

Week of Proper 11

Mon
1 Exod. 14:5–18   C8 *or* Ps. 114   Matt. 12:38–42
2 Micah 6:1–8   Ps. 14   Matt. 12:38–42

Tue
1 Exod. 14:21–15:1   C8 *or* Ps. 114   Matt. 12:46–50
2 Micah 7:14–15,18–20   Ps. 85:1–7   Matt. 12:46–50

Wed
1 Exod. 16:1–5,9–15   Ps. 78:18–29   Matt. 13:1–9
2 Jer. 1:1,4–10   Ps. 71:1–6,15–17   Matt. 13:1–9

Thu
1 Exod. 19:1–20   C13 *or* Ps. 24:1–6   Matt. 13:10–17
2 Jer. 2:1–3,7–13   Ps. 36:5–10   Matt. 13:10–17

Fri
1 Exod. 20:1–17   Ps. 19:7–10   Matt. 13:18–23
2 Jer. 3:14–18   Ps. 121   Matt. 13:18–23

Sat
1 Exod. 24:3–8   Ps. 51:11–16   Matt. 13:24–30
2 Jer. 7:1–11   Ps. 84   Matt. 13:24–30

Week of Proper 12

Mon
1 Exod. 32:15–24,30–34   Ps. 106:19–23   Matt. 13:31–35
2 Jer. 13:1–11   Ps. 95   Matt. 13:31–35

Tue
1 Exod. 33:7–11;   Ps. 103:5–13   Matt. 13:36–43
   34:5–10, 27–28
2 Jer. 14:17–22   Ps. 79:9–13   Matt. 13:36–43

Wed
1 Exod. 34:29–35   Ps. 99   Matt. 13:44–46
2 Jer. 15:10,15–21   Ps. 59:1–4,18–20   Matt. 13:44–46

Thu
1 Exod. 40:16–21,34–38   Ps. 84   Matt. 13:47–53
2 Jer. 18:1–6   Ps. 146:1–5   Matt. 13:47–53

Fri
1 Lev. 23:1–11,26–38   Ps. 81:1–10   Matt. 13:54–58
2 Jer. 26:1–9   Ps. 70   Matt. 13:54–58

Sat
1 Lev. 25:1,8–17   Ps. 67   Matt. 14:1–12
2 Jer. 26:11–16,24   Ps. 140:1–5   Matt. 14:1–12

Week of Proper 13

Mon

1 Num. 11:4–15 Ps. 105:37–45 Matt. 14:22–36
2 Jer. 28:1–17 Ps. 119:89–96 Matt. 14:13–21

Tue

1 Num. 12:1–16 Ps. 51:1–12 Matt. 15:1–2,10–14
2 Jer. 30:1–2,12–22 Ps. 102:16–22 Matt. 14:22–36

Wed

1 Num. 13:1–2,25– Ps. 106:6–14,21–23 Matt. 15:21–28
  14:1,26–35
2 Jer. 31:1–7 Ps. 121 Matt. 15:21–28

Thu

1 Num. 20:1–13 Ps. 95:1–9 Matt. 16:13–23
2 Jer. 31:31–34 Ps. 51:11–18 Matt. 16:13–23

Fri

1 Deut. 4:32–40 Ps. 105:1–6 Matt. 16:24–28
2 Nahum 1:15;2:2; Ps. 124 Matt. 16:24–28
  3:1–3,6–7

Sat

1 Deut. 6:4–13 Ps. 18:1–2,48–50 Matt. 17:14–20
2 Hab. 1:12–2:4 Ps. 9:7–12 Matt. 17:14–20

Week of Proper 14

Mon

1 Deut. 10:12–22	Ps. 148	Matt. 17:22–27
2 Ezek. 1:1–5,24–28	Ps. 148:1–4,13–14	Matt. 17:22–27

Tue

1 Deut. 31:1–8	Ps. 111	Matt. 18:1–5, 10,12–14
2 Ezek. 2:8–3:4	Ps. 119:65–72	Matt. 18:1–5, 10,12–14

Wed

1 Deut. 34:1–12	Ps. 66:1–8	Matt. 18:15–20
2 Ezek. 9:1–7;10:18–22	Ps. 113	Matt. 18:15–20

Thu

1 Joshua 3:7–17	Ps. 114	Matt. 18:21–19:1
2 Ezek. 12:1–16	Ps. 39:11–15	Matt. 18:21–19:1

Fri

1 Joshua 24:1–13	Ps. 136:1–3,16–22	Matt. 19:3–12
2 Ezek. 16:1–15,59–63	C10 *or* Ps. 11	Matt. 19:3–12

Sat

1 Joshua 24:14–29	Ps. 16:1,5–11	Matt. 19:13–15
2 Ezek. 18:1–13,30–32	Ps. 51:11–18	Matt. 19:13–15

Week of Proper 15

Mon

1 Judges 2:11–19	Ps. 51:1–10	Matt. 19:16–22
2 Ezek. 24:15–24	Ps. 79:1–8	Matt. 19:16–22

Tue

1 Judges 5:11–24a	Ps. 85:8–13	Matt. 19:23–30
2 Ezek. 28:1–10	Ps. 60:1–5	Matt. 19:23–30

Wed

1 Judges 9:6–15	Ps. 21:1–6	Matt. 20:1–16a
2 Ezek. 34:1–11	Ps. 23	Matt. 20:1–16a

Thu

1 Judges 13:1–7	Ps. 139:10–17	Matt. 22:1–14
2 Ezek. 36:22–28	Ps. 51:8–13	Matt. 22:1–14

Fri

1 Ruth 1:1–22	Ps. 146	Matt. 22:34–40
2 Ezek. 37:1–14	Ps. 107:1–8	Matt. 22:34–40

Sat

1 Ruth 2:1–11;4:13–17	Ps. 128	Matt. 23:1–12
2 Ezek. 43:1–7	Ps. 85:8–13	Matt. 23:1–12

Week of Proper 16

Mon
1 1 Thess. 1:1–10   Ps. 149:1–5   Matt. 23:13–22
2 2 Thess. 1:1–5,11–12   Ps. 96:1–5   Matt. 23:13–22

Tue
1 1 Thess. 2:1–8   Ps. 139:1–9   Matt. 23:23–26
2 2 Thess. 2:1–17   Ps. 96:7–13   Matt. 23:23–26

Wed
1 1 Thess. 2:9–13   Ps. 126   Matt. 23:27–32
2 2 Thess. 3:6–10,16–18   Ps. 128   Matt. 23:27–32

Thu
1 1 Thess. 3:6–13   Ps. 90:13–17   Matt. 24:42–51
2 1 Cor. 1:1–9   Ps. 145:1–7   Matt. 24:42–51

Fri
1 1 Thess. 4:1–8   Ps. 97   Matt. 25:1–13
2 1 Cor. 1:17–25   Ps. 33:1–11   Matt. 25:1–13

Sat
1 1 Thess. 4:9–12   Ps. 98   Matt. 25:14–30
2 1 Cor. 1:26–31   Ps. 33:12–22   Matt. 25:14–30

Week of Proper 17

Mon

1 1 Thess. 4:13–18　　Ps. 96　　　　　　Luke 4:16–30
2 1 Cor. 2:1–5　　　　Ps. 119:97–103　　Luke 4:16–30

Tue

1 1 Thess. 5:1–11　　 Ps. 27:1–6,17–18　Luke 4:31–37
2 1 Cor. 2:10–16　　　Ps. 145:8–15　　　Luke 4:31–37

Wed

1 Col. 1:1–8　　　　　Ps. 34:9–22　　　　Luke 4:38–44
2 1 Cor. 3:1–9　　　　Ps. 62　　　　　　　Luke 4:38–44

Thu

1 Col. 1:9–14　　　　 Ps. 98　　　　　　　Luke 5:1–11
2 1 Cor. 3:18–23　　　Ps. 24:1–6　　　　　Luke 5:1–11

Fri

1 Col. 1:15–20　　　　Ps. 100　　　　　　 Luke 5:33–39
2 1 Cor. 4:1–5　　　　Ps. 37:1–12　　　　 Luke 5:33–39

Sat

1 Col. 1:21–23　　　　Ps. 54　　　　　　　Luke 6:1–5
2 1 Cor. 4:6–15　　　　Ps. 145:14–22　　　Luke 6:1–5

Week of Proper 18

Mon
1 Col. 1:24–2:3   Ps. 62:1–7   Luke 6:6–11
2 1 Cor. 5:1–8   Ps. 5   Luke 6:6–11

Tue
1 Col. 2:6–15   Ps. 145:1–9   Luke 6:12–19
2 1 Cor. 6:1–11   Ps. 149:1–5   Luke 6:12–19

Wed
1 Col. 3:1–11   Ps. 145:10–13   Luke 6:20–26
2 1 Cor. 7:25–31   Ps. 47   Luke 6:20–26

Thu
1 Col. 3:12–17   Ps. 150   Luke 6:27–38
2 1 Cor. 8:1–13   Ps. 139:1–9,22–23   Luke 6:27–38

Fri
1 1 Tim. 1:1–2,12–14   Ps. 16   Luke 6:39–42
2 1 Cor. 9:16–27   Ps. 84   Luke 6:39–42

Sat
1 1 Tim. 1:15–17   Ps. 113   Luke 6:43–49
2 1 Cor. 10:14–22   Ps. 116:10–17   Luke 6:43–49

Week of Proper 19

Mon
1 1 Tim. 2:1–8　　　　　Ps. 28　　　　　　　Luke 7:1–10
2 1 Cor. 11:17–28,33　　Ps. 40:8–12　　　　 Luke 7:1–10

Tue
1 1 Tim. 3:1–13　　　　　　Ps. 101　　　　　　Luke 7:11–17
2 1 Cor. 12:12–14,27–31　　Ps. 100　　　　　　Luke 7:11–17

Wed
1 1 Tim. 3:14–16　　　　　Ps. 111:1–6　　　　Luke 7:31–35
2 1 Cor. 12:31–13:13　　　Ps. 33:1–12,22　　 Luke 7:31–35

Thu
1 1 Tim. 4:12–16　　　　Ps. 111:7–10　　　　Luke 7:36–50
2 1 Cor. 15:1–11　　　　 Ps. 118:14–29　　　Luke 7:36–50

Fri
1 1 Tim. 6:1–12　　　　　Ps. 49:1–9　　　　　Luke 8:1–3
2 1 Cor. 15:12–20　　　　Ps. 17:1–7　　　　　Luke 8:1–3

Sat
1 1 Tim. 6:13–16　　　　Ps. 100　　　　　　　Luke 8:4–15
2 1 Cor. 15:35–49　　　　Ps. 30:1–5　　　　　Luke 8:4–15

Week of Proper 20

Mon
1 Ezra 1:1–6	Ps. 126	Luke 8:16–18
2 Prov. 3:27–35	Ps. 15	Luke 8:16–18

Tue
1 Ezra 6:1–8,12–19	Ps. 124	Luke 8:19–21
2 Prov. 21:1–6,10–13	Ps. 119:1–8	Luke 8:19–21

Wed
1 Ezra 9:5–9	C11 *or* Ps. 48	Luke 9:1–6
2 Prov. 30:5–9	Ps. 24:1–6	Luke 9:1–6

Thu
1 Haggai 1:1–8	Ps. 149:1–5	Luke 9:7–9
2 Eccles. 1:1–11	Ps. 90:1–6	Luke 9:7–9

Fri
1 Haggai 1:15b—2:9	Ps. 43	Luke 9:18–22
2 Eccles. 3:1–11	Ps. 144:1–4	Luke 9:18–22

Sat
1 Zech. 2:1–11	Ps. 121	Luke 9:43b–45
2 Eccles. 11:9–12:8	Ps. 90:1–2,12–17	Luke 9:43b–45

Week of Proper 21

Mon
1 Zech. 8:1–8   Ps. 102:11–22   Luke 9:46–50
2 Job 1:6–22   Ps. 17:1–7   Luke 9:46–50

Tue
1 Zech. 8:20–23   Ps. 87   Luke 9:51–56
2 Job 3:1–3,11–23   Ps. 88:1–8   Luke 9:51–56

Wed
1 Neh. 2:1–8   Ps. 137:1–6   Luke 9:57–62
2 Job 9:1–16   Ps. 88:10–15   Luke 9:57–62

Thu
1 Neh. 8:1–12   Ps. 119:1–8   Luke 10:1–12
2 Job 19:21–27   Ps. 27:10–18   Luke 10:1–12

Fri
1 Baruch 1:15–21   Ps. 79:1–9   Luke 10:13–16
2 Job 38:1,12–21;40:1–5 Ps. 139:1–17   Luke 10:13–16

Sat
1 Baruch 4:5–12,27–29   Ps. 69:34–38   Luke 10:17–24
2 Job 42:1–6,12–17   Ps. 119:169–176   Luke 10:17–24

Week of Proper 22

Mon
1 Jonah 1:1–17;2:10   Ps. 130   Luke 10:25–37
2 Gal. 1:6–12   Ps. 111:1–6   Luke 10:25–37

Tue
1 Jonah 3:1–10   Ps. 6   Luke 10:38–42
2 Gal. 1:13–24   Ps. 139:1–14   Luke 10:38–42

Wed
1 Jonah 4:1–11   Ps. 86:1–10   Luke 11:1–4
2 Gal. 2:1–2,7–14   Ps. 117   Luke 11:1–4

Thu
1 Mal. 3:13–4:2a   Ps. 1   Luke 11:5–13
2 Gal. 3:1–5   C16 *or*   Luke 11:5–13
                         Ps. 89:19–29

Fri
1 Joel 1:13–15;2:1–2   Ps. 9:1–8   Luke 11:14–26
2 Gal. 3:7–14   Ps. 111:4–10   Luke 11:14–26

Sat
1 Joel 3:12–21   Ps. 97   Luke 11:27–28
2 Gal. 3:21–29   Ps. 105:1–7   Luke 11:27–28

Week of Proper 23

Mon
1 Rom. 1:1–7   Ps. 98   Luke 11:29–32
2 Gal. 4:21–5:1   Ps. 138   Luke 11:29–32

Tue
1 Rom. 1:16–25   Ps. 19:1–4   Luke 11:37–41
2 Gal. 5:1–6   Ps. 119:41–48   Luke 11:37–41

Wed
1 Rom. 2:1–11   Ps. 62:1–9   Luke 11:42–46
2 Gal. 6:1–10   Ps. 32   Luke 11:42–46

Thu
1 Rom. 3:21–31   Ps. 130   Luke 11:47–54
2 Eph. 1:1–10   Ps. 98   Luke 11:47–54

Fri
1 Rom. 4:1–8   Ps. 32   Luke 12:1–7
2 Eph. 1:11–14   Ps. 33:1–12   Luke 12:1–7

Sat
1 Rom. 4:13–18   Ps. 105:5–10,42–45 Luke 12:8–12
2 Eph. 1:15–23   Ps. 8   Luke 12:8–12

Week of Proper 24

Mon

1 Rom. 4:13,19–25	C16 *or* Ps. 89:19–29	Luke 12:13–21
2 Eph. 2:1–10	Ps. 100	Luke 12:13–21

Tue

1 Rom. 5:6–21	Ps. 40:8–11	Luke 12:35–38
2 Eph. 2:11–22	Ps. 85:8–13	Luke 12:35–38

Wed

1 Rom. 6:12–18	Ps. 124	Luke 12:39–48
2 Eph. 3:4–12	C9 *or* Ps. 113 *or* Ps. 122	Luke 12:39–48

Thu

1 Rom. 6:19–23	Ps. 1	Luke 12:49–53
2 Eph. 3:14–21	Ps. 33:1–11	Luke 12:49–53

Fri

1 Rom. 7:18–25a	Ps. 19:7–14	Luke 12:54–59
2 Eph. 4:1–6	Ps. 24:1–6	Luke 12:54–59

Sat

1 Rom. 8:1–11	Ps. 24:1–6	Luke 13:1–9
2 Eph. 4:7–16	Ps. 122	Luke 13:1–9

Week of Proper 25

Mon

1 Rom. 8:12–17	Ps. 68:1–6,19–20	Luke 13:10–17
2 Eph. 5:1–8	Ps. 37:27–33	Luke 13:10–17

Tue

1 Rom. 8:18–25	Ps. 126	Luke 13:18–21
2 Eph. 5:21–33	Ps. 128	Luke 13:18–21

Wed

1 Rom. 8:26–30	Ps. 91:9–16	Luke 13:22–30
2 Eph. 6:1–9	Ps. 145:10–19	Luke 13:22–30

Thu

1 Rom. 8:31–39	Ps. 30	Luke 13:31–35
2 Eph. 6:10–20	Ps. 144:1–10	Luke 13:31–35

Fri

1 Rom. 9:1–5	Ps. 147:13–21	Luke 14:1–6
2 Phil. 1:1–11	Ps. 111	Luke 14:1–6

Sat

1 Rom. 11:1–6,11–12, 25–29	Ps. 94:14–19	Luke 14:1,7–11
2 Phil. 1:12–26	Ps. 42:1–7	Luke 14:1,7–11

Week of Proper 26

Mon
1 Rom. 11:29–36   Ps. 16:5–11   Luke 14:12–14
2 Phil. 2:1–4   Ps. 131   Luke 14:12–14

Tue
1 Rom. 12:1–16   Ps. 131   Luke 14:15–24
2 Phil. 2:5–11   Ps. 22:22–28 Luke 14:15–24

Wed
1 Rom. 13:8–10   Ps. 112   Luke 14:25–33
2 Phil. 2:12–18   Ps. 62:6–14   Luke 14:25–33

Thu
1 Rom. 14:7–12   Ps. 27:1–6,17–18   Luke 15:1–10
2 Phil. 3:3–8a   Ps. 105:1–7   Luke 15:1–10

Fri
1 Rom. 15:14–21   Ps. 98   Luke 16:1–8
2 Phil. 3:17–4:1 Ps. 122   Luke 16:1–8

Sat
1 Rom. 16:3–9,16,22–27   Ps. 145:1–7   Luke 16:9–15
2 Phil. 4:10–19   Ps. 112   Luke 16:9–15

Week of Proper 27

Mon

1 Wisdom 1:1–7	Ps. 139:1–9	Luke 17:1–6
2 Titus 1:1–9	Ps. 24:1–6	Luke 17:1–6

Tue

1 Wisdom 2:23–3:9	Ps. 34:15–22	Luke 17:7–10
2 Titus 2:1–14	Ps. 37:1–6,28–29	Luke 17:7–10

Wed

1 Wisdom 6:1–11	Ps. 2	Luke 17:11–19
2 Titus 3:1–7	Ps. 91:9–16	Luke 17:11–19

Thu

1 Wisdom 7:21–8:1	Ps. 119:89–96	Luke 17:20–25
2 Philemon 1,4–20	Ps. 146	Luke 17:20–25

Fri

1 Wisdom 13:1–9	Ps. 19:1–4	Luke 17:26–37
2 2 John 4–9	Ps. 119:1–8	Luke 17:26–37

Sat

1 Wisdom 18:14–16; 19:6–9	Ps. 105:1–6,37–45	Luke 18:1–8
2 3 John 5–8	Ps. 112	Luke 18:1–8

Week of Proper 28

Mon

1 1 Macc. 1:1–15,54–57, 62–64 Ps. 79 Luke 18:35–43

2 Rev. 1:1–4;2:1–5 Ps. 1 Luke 18:35–43

Tue

1 2 Macc. 6:18–31 Ps. 3 Luke 19:1–10

2 Rev. 3:1–6,14–22 Ps. 15 Luke 19:1–10

Wed

1 2 Macc. 7:1,20–31, 39–42 Ps. 17:1–8 Luke 19:11–28

2 Rev. 4:1–11 Ps. 150 Luke 19:11–28

Thu

1 1 Macc. 2:15–29 Ps. 129 Luke 19:41–44

2 Rev. 5:1–10 Ps. 149:1–5 Luke 19:41–44

Fri

1 1 Macc. 4:36–37,52–59 C9 *or* Ps. 113 *or* Ps. 122 Luke 19:45–48

2 Rev. 10:8–11 Ps. 119:65–72 Luke 19:45–48

Sat

1 1 Macc. 6:1–13 Ps. 124 Luke 20:27–40

2 Rev. 11:1–12 Ps. 144:1–10 Luke 20:27–40

Week of the Last Sunday after Pentecost—Proper 29

Mon

1 Dan. 1:1–20	C13 *or* Ps. 24:1–6	Luke 21:1–4
2 Rev. 14:1–5	Ps. 24:1–6	Luke 21:1–4

Tue

1 Dan. 2:31–45	C12 part I *or* Ps. 96	Luke 21:5–9
2 Rev. 14:14–20	Ps. 96	Luke 21:5–9

Wed

1 Dan. 5:1–6,13–28	C12 part I *or* Ps. 98	Luke 21:10–19
2 Rev. 15:1–4	Ps. 98	Luke 21:10–19

Thu

1 Dan. 6:6–27	C12 part I *or* Ps. 99	Luke 21:20–28
2 Rev. 18:1–2,21–19:3,9	Ps. 100	Luke 21:20–28

Fri

1 Dan. 7:1–14	C12 part II *or* Ps. 97	Luke 21:29–33
2 Rev. 20:1–4,11–21:4	Ps. 84	Luke 21:29–33

Sat

1 Dan. 7:15–27	C12 part III *or* Ps. 95:1–7	Luke 21:34–36
2 Rev. 22:1–7	Ps. 95:1–7	Luke 21:34–36

A Six-Week Eucharistic Lectionary with Daily Themes and Suggested Collects

(Adapted from Weekday Readings, a daily lectionary authorized by the 1994 General Convention)

Concerning the Lectionary

This Lectionary offers thirty-six sets of thematic readings intended for use on the weekdays following the First Sunday after the Epiphany and the Day of Pentecost. These readings may be used in sequence or as a corpus of texts and themes available in whatever order the celebrant and worshiping community wish to use them.

Each Proper includes two brief lessons and a psalm; the psalm reflects the theme of the two lessons. The brevity of the readings invites a brief reflective homily, silence, or the reading of non-biblical meditative material.

The suggested collects, with the page numbers for their traditional and contemporary forms, are from the Book of Common Prayer.

Week One

Monday—*The commandment of love*
Collect: Proper 9 (179 / 230) or 7 Epiphany (164 / 216)

| Rom. 13:8–10 | Ps. 85:7–13 | Luke 6:32–36 |

Tuesday—*The family of God*
Collect: 14. For the Unity of the Church (204 / 255)

| Eph. 4:29–32 | Ps. 42:1–7 | Matt. 12:46–50 |

Wednesday—*The power of prayer*
Collect: 6 Epiphany (164 / 216)

| James 5:13–18 | Ps. 111:1–10 | Luke 11:9–13 |

Thursday—*The commandments of the covenant*
Collect: Proper 9 (179 / 230)

| Deut. 6:4–7 | Ps. 119:1–6 | Matt. 22:34–40 |

Friday—*The promise of the cross*
Collect: 6. Of the Holy Cross (201 / 252)

| Rom. 8:35,37–39 | Ps. 23 | Mark 8:31–33 |

Saturday—*Sabbath celebration; Creation and Word*
Collect: A Collect for Saturdays (56 / 99) or First Sunday after Christmas (161 / 213)

| Gen. 1:31–2:3 | Ps. 104:25–32 | John 1:1–5,12–14, 16–18 |

Week Two

Monday—Christian humility
Collect: Proper 18 (181 / 233)
1 Pet. 5:5b–7	Ps. 147:5–12	Mark 9:33–37

Tuesday—God's wisdom, an unfolding mystery
Collect: 2. Of the Holy Spirit (200 / 251)
1 Cor. 2:6–10a	Ps. 49:1–11	Matt. 13:31–33

Wednesday—Dress code for the disciple
Collect: 1 Advent (159 / 211)
Eph. 6:10–18	Ps. 1	Mark 6:6b–13

Thursday—The power of our baptism
Collect: 10. At Baptism (203 / 254)
1 Pet. 1:3–5;2:9–10	Ps. 96:1–9	John 9:1,5–11

Friday—The role of the servant/disciple
Collect: A Collect for Fridays (56 / 99)
Isa. 53:11–12	Ps. 66:7–11	Luke 9:18–26

Saturday—God known in creative power
Collect: Proper 3 (177 / 229)
Job 38:1,4–14,16–18	Ps. 33:6–11	Mark 4:35–41

Week Three

Monday—Leaving judgment to God
Collect: 8 Epiphany (165 / 216)
James 4:11–12   Ps. 24:1–6   John 12:44–50

Tuesday—Discipleship seen in justice toward the poor
Collect: 21. For Social Justice (209 / 260) or 22. For Social Service (209 / 260)
Lev. 19:1–2,9–14   Ps. 22:22–26   Luke 14:12–14

Wednesday—Standards for the Church
Collect: Proper 15 (180 / 232)
Rom. 12:14–21   Ps. 146   John 15:11–17

Thursday—Living for the kingdom of God
Collect: 6 Easter (174 / 225)
Gal. 6:14–16   Ps. 67   Matt. 13:44–46

Friday—The cost of discipleship
Collect: A Collect for Fridays (56 / 99)
Jer. 20:7–9   Ps. 13:1–6   Matt. 10:34–39

Saturday—The significance of the Sabbath
Collect: A Collect for Saturdays (56 / 99)
Exod. 20:8–11   Ps. 145:10–18   Mark 2:23–28

Week Four

Monday—Enduring trials for the sake of the gospel
Collect: 6. Of the Holy Cross (202 / 252)
2 Cor. 11:21b–33   Ps. 55:1–7   Luke 6:20–26

Tuesday—A foretaste of the kingdom of God
Collect: Proper 20 (182 / 234)
Rev. 21:1–4   Ps. 47   Matt. 11:2–6

Wednesday—The Church sanctified in God's truth
Collect: Proper 24 (183 / 235)
Eph. 3:14–19   Ps. 122   John 17:1–8,17–18

Thursday—Responding to God's revelation in Christ
Collect: Proper 17 (181 / 233)
Rom. 12:1–8   Ps. 34:1–6   John 14:8–14

Friday—The power of witness
Collect: Of a Saint 3 (199 / 250)
Heb. 12:1–4,12–14   Ps. 27:1–7   Matt. 27:50–51,54

Saturday—The sabbath; living as God's new creations
Collect: A Collect for Saturdays (56 / 99)
2 Cor. 5:14–21   Ps. 148   Luke 12:22–31

Week Five

Monday—*Gifts of the gospel*
Collect: 4 Lent (167 / 219)
Eph. 1:15–23   Ps. 98   John 6:35–40,47–51

Tuesday—*Christ dwelling in us*
Collect: 4. Of the Incarnation (200 / 252)
Col. 3:16–17   Ps. 132:8–15   John 17:20–26

Wednesday—*Living in faith and confidence*
Collect: Proper 2 (177 / 228)
Exod. 33:12–17   Ps. 25:3–9   Matt. 10:26–31

Thursday—*God's continuing revelation*
Collect: 2. Of the Holy Spirit (200 / 251)
Rom. 16:25–27   Ps. 112   John 16:12–15

Friday—*The power of the cross*
Collect: A Collect for Fridays (56 / 99)
Rom. 3:21–26   Ps. 15   Mark 14:22–25

Saturday—*Sabbath: a time for discernment*
Collect: Proper 10 (179 / 231)
1 Kings 19:8–13a   Ps. 65:9–14   Mark 1:35–39

Week Six

Monday—The Christian calling: reflecting God's justice
Collect: 21. For Social Justice (209 / 260)
Amos 5:21–24 Ps. 50:7–15 Luke 4:14–21

Tuesday—A woman's offering
Collect: Proper 17 (181 / 233)
1 Sam. 1:9–11 Ps. 33:12–22 Mark 12:38–44

Wednesday—The Church as window to God's nature
Collect: Proper 21 (182 / 234)
Exod. 34:6–7 Ps. 130 Luke 6:37–38

Thursday—The gift of baptism
Collect: Collect at the Easter Vigil, following Isa. 55:1–11 (290)
Gal. 3:27–29 Ps. 84:1–8 John 4:13–15

Friday—Dying in order to be born
Collect: A Collect for Fridays (56 / 99)
Gal. 2:19b–20 Ps. 126 John 12:20–26

Saturday—Sabbath rest
Collect: A Collect for Saturdays (56 / 99)
Heb. 4:9–11 Ps. 29:1–10 Luke 23:50–56

3. The Sanctoral Cycle: Commemorations of Saints

Introduction

The Baptismal Covenant grounds the theology of the Book of Common Prayer. All those baptized into Christ participate in the same risen life with him and together form the mystical Body of Christ that is the Church. In the Prayers of the People at each Eucharist, we lift up to God the whole state of Christ's Church; in addition to praying for those living, we pray for all who have died and pray that we may share with all the saints in God's eternal kingdom. In baptism, we are joined with Christ in bonds that cannot be broken—even by death. Those who sleep in Christ are not just part of the Church of the past, they are part of the Church of the present as well.

From its earliest days the Church has rejoiced to recognize and commemorate those faithful departed who were extraordinary or even heroic servants of God and of God's people for the sake, and after the example, of their Savior Jesus Christ. By this recognition and commemoration, their devoted service endures in the Spirit, even as their example and fellowship continue to nurture the pilgrim Church on its way to God.

There are a variety of views concerning who and what a saint is: some would identify a saint as any Christian who has struggled to lead a faithful life; others reserve the title for those who have demonstrated heroic virtue on account of their depth of union with Christ and who now participate in the nearer presence of God. There are also a variety of views concerning how the saints relate to the present church: some see them as figures of the past who have left us good examples of leading the Christian life; others see them as present participants in the life of Church, still engaged in the Church's ministry of intercession for ourselves and the world.

When a local community decides to commemorate a particular historical individual, whether he or she is included in *A Great Cloud of Witnesses: A Calendar of Commemorations* or not, the materials here provide the propers necessary for the celebration. For each individual found in *A Great Cloud of Witnesses*, that resource offers a collect and indicates the proper preface to be used at the Eucharist. For individuals not found in *A Great Cloud of Witnesses*, an appropriate Common of Saints selected from this resource can provide a collect and indicate which proper preface to use. In either case, appropriate readings may be selected from among the Commons that most closely reflect the saint's life, work, and witness.

For some Episcopalians, an important part of the lively experience of the saints consists of praying alongside them. The principle of Christ as the sole mediator between humanity and God is a deep and important one within our tradition; prayer alongside the saints does not and should not compromise this principle in any way. Rather, praying alongside the saints grows out of the importance of baptism and taking seriously the implications of a baptismal ecclesiology.

The Daily Office and the Sanctoral Cycle

On the one hand, saints were historically honored in the pre-Reformation Church in the Office, providing centuries of precedent for continuing this custom. On the other hand, the number and type of sanctoral celebrations eventually obscured the praying of the full Psalter and continually interrupted the reading of Scripture. Thomas Cranmer lamented this situation in the preface to the first Book of Common Prayer (1549; see BCP 1979, 866). Remembering the saints in the Office is certainly appropriate as long as it does not take away from the continuous reading of Scripture or obscure the rhythms of the temporal cycle.

The readings appointed within this resource are for use at the Eucharist and for devotional reading. They are not intended to displace the readings appointed for the Daily Office.

The collect provided for a Day of Optional Observance may be used as the Collect of the Day in the Office at the discretion of the officiant. When a sanctoral collect is used in the Office as the Collect of the Day, the collect of the preceding Sunday or Principal Feast may be used after the Collect of the Day in order to maintain a connection with the Church's seasons.

The Common of Saints from the Book of Common Prayer

Concerning the Common of Saints

The festival of a saint is observed in accordance with the rules of precedence set forth in the Calendar of the church year.

At the discretion of the Celebrant, and as appropriate, one of the following Commons may be used

a) at the commemoration of a saint listed in the Calendar, in place of the Proper for Lesser Feasts

b) at the patronal festival or commemoration of a saint not listed in the Calendar.

Any of the sets of Lessons assigned to a given Common may be used with any of the Collects.

Common of a Martyr I

I O Almighty God, who didst give to thy servant N. boldness to confess the Name of our Savior Jesus Christ before the rulers of this world, and courage to die for this faith: Grant that we may always be ready to give a reason for the hope that is in us, and to suffer gladly for the sake of the same our Lord Jesus Christ; who liveth and reigneth with thee and the Holy Spirit, one God, for ever and ever. *Amen.*

II Almighty God, who gave to your servant N. boldness to confess the Name of our Savior Jesus Christ before the rulers of this world, and courage to die for this faith: Grant that we may always be ready to give a reason for the hope that is in us, and to suffer gladly for the sake of our Lord Jesus Christ; who lives and reigns with you and the Holy Spirit, one God, for ever and ever. *Amen.*

Psalm	Lessons
126	2 Esdras 2:42–48
or 121	1 Peter 3:14–18,22
	Matthew 10:16–22

Preface of a Saint

Common of a Martyr II

I O Almighty God, by whose grace and power thy holy martyr N. triumphed over suffering and was faithful even unto death: Grant us, who now remember *him* with thanksgiving, to be so faithful in our witness to thee in this world, that we may receive with *him* the crown of life; through Jesus Christ our Lord, who liveth and reigneth with thee and the Holy Spirit, one God, for ever and ever. *Amen.*

II Almighty God, by whose grace and power your holy martyr N. triumphed over suffering and was faithful even to death: Grant us, who now remember *him* in thanksgiving, to be so faithful in our witness to you in this world, that we may receive with *him* the crown of life; through Jesus Christ our Lord, who lives and reigns with you and the Holy Spirit, one God, for ever and ever. *Amen.*

Psalm	Lessons
116	Sirach (Ecclesiasticus) 51:1–12
or 116:1–8	Revelation 7:13–17
	Luke 12:2–12

Preface of a Saint

Common of a Martyr III

I Almighty and everlasting God, who didst enkindle the flame of thy love in the heart of thy holy martyr N.: Grant to us, thy humble servants, a like faith and power of love, that we who rejoice in *her* triumph may profit by *her* example; through Jesus Christ our Lord, who liveth and reigneth with thee and the Holy Spirit, one God, for ever and ever. *Amen.*

II Almighty and everlasting God, who kindled the flame of your love in the heart of your holy martyr N.: Grant to us, your humble servants, a like faith and power of love, that we who rejoice in *her* triumph may profit by *her* example; through Jesus Christ our Lord, who lives and reigns with you and the Holy Spirit, one God, for ever and ever. *Amen.*

Psalm	**Lessons**
124	Jeremiah 15:15–21
or 31:1–5	1 Peter 4:12–19
	Mark 8:34–38

Preface of a Saint

Common of a Missionary I

I   Almighty and everlasting God, we thank thee for thy servant N., whom thou didst call to preach the Gospel to the people of_____ (or to the_____ people). Raise up, we beseech thee, in this and every land evangelists and heralds of thy kingdom, that thy Church may proclaim the unsearchable riches of our Savior Jesus Christ; who liveth and reigneth with thee and the Holy Spirit, one God, now and for ever. *Amen.*

II Almighty and everlasting God, we thank you for your servant N., whom you called to preach the Gospel to the people of_____ (or to the_____ people). Raise up in this and every land evangelists and heralds of your kingdom, that your Church may proclaim the unsearchable riches of our Savior Jesus Christ; who lives and reigns with you and the Holy Spirit, one God, now and for ever. *Amen.*

Psalm	Lessons
96	Isaiah 52:7–10
or 96:1–7	Acts 1:1–9
	Luke 10:1–9

Preface of Pentecost

Common of a Missionary II

I Almighty God, who willest to be glorified in thy saints, and didst raise up thy servant N. to be a light in the world: Shine, we pray thee, in our hearts, that we also in our generation may show forth thy praise, who hast called us out of darkness into thy marvelous light; through Jesus Christ our Lord, who liveth and reigneth with thee and the Holy Spirit, one God, now and for ever. *Amen.*

II Almighty God, whose will it is to be glorified in your saints, and who raised up your servant N. to be a light in the world: Shine, we pray, in our hearts, that we also in our generation may show forth your praise, who called us out of darkness into your marvelous light; through Jesus Christ our Lord, who lives and reigns with you and the Holy Spirit, one God, now and for ever. *Amen.*

Psalm	**Lessons**
98	Isaiah 49:1–6
or 98:1–4	Acts 17:22–31
	Matthew 28:16–20

Preface of Pentecost

Common of a Pastor I

I O heavenly Father, Shepherd of thy people, we give thee thanks for thy servant N., who was faithful in the care and nurture of thy flock; and we pray that, following *his* example and the teaching of *his* holy life, we may by thy grace grow into the stature of the fullness of our Lord and Savior Jesus Christ; who liveth and reigneth with thee and the Holy Spirit, one God, for ever and ever. *Amen.*

II Heavenly Father, Shepherd of your people, we thank you for your servant N., who was faithful in the care and nurture of your flock; and we pray that, following *his* example and the teaching of *his* holy life, we may by your grace grow into the stature of the fullness of our Lord and Savior Jesus Christ; who lives and reigns with you and the Holy Spirit, one God, for ever and ever. *Amen.*

Psalm	**Lessons**
23	Ezekiel 34:11–16
	1 Peter 5:1–4
	John 21:15–17

Preface of a Saint

Common of a Pastor II

I O God, our heavenly Father, who didst raise up thy faithful servant N. to be a [bishop and] pastor in thy Church and to feed thy flock: Give abundantly to all pastors the gifts of thy Holy Spirit, that they may minister in thy household as true servants of Christ and stewards of thy divine mysteries; through the same Jesus Christ our Lord, who liveth and reigneth with thee and the same Spirit, one God, for ever and ever. *Amen.*

II O God, our heavenly Father, who raised up your faithful servant N., to be a [bishop and] pastor in your Church and to feed your flock: Give abundantly to all pastors the gifts of your Holy Spirit, that they may minister in your household as true servants of Christ and stewards of your divine mysteries; through Jesus Christ our Lord, who lives and reigns with you and the Holy Spirit, one God, for ever and ever. *Amen.*

Psalm	**Lessons**
84	Acts 20:17–35
or 84:7–11	Ephesians 3:14–21
	Matthew 24:42–47

Preface of a Saint

Common of a Theologian and Teacher I

I O God, who by thy Holy Spirit dost give to some the word of wisdom, to others the word of knowledge, and to others the word of faith: We praise thy Name for the gifts of grace manifested in thy servant N., and we pray that thy Church may never be destitute of such gifts; through Jesus Christ our Lord, who with thee and the same Spirit liveth and reigneth, one God, for ever and ever. *Amen.*

II O God, by your Holy Spirit you give to some the word of wisdom, to others the word of knowledge, and to others the word of faith: We praise your Name for the gifts of grace manifested in your servant N., and we pray that your Church may never be destitute of such gifts; through Jesus Christ our Lord, who with you and the Holy Spirit lives and reigns, one God, for ever and ever. *Amen.*

Psalm	Lessons
119:97–104	Wisdom 7:7–14
	1 Corinthians 2:6–10,13–16
	John 17:18–23

Preface of a Saint, or of Trinity Sunday

Common of a Theologian and Teacher II

I O Almighty God, who didst give to thy servant N. special gifts of grace to understand and teach the truth as it is in Christ Jesus: Grant, we beseech thee, that by this teaching we may know thee, the one true God, and Jesus Christ whom thou hast sent; who liveth and reigneth with thee and the Holy Spirit, one God, for ever and ever. *Amen.*

II Almighty God, you gave to your servant N. special gifts of grace to understand and teach the truth as it is in Christ Jesus: Grant that by this teaching we may know you, the one true God, and Jesus Christ whom you have sent; who lives and reigns with you and the Holy Spirit, one God, for ever and ever. *Amen.*

Psalm

119:89–96

Lessons

Proverbs 3:1–7
1 Corinthians 3:5–11
Matthew 13:47–52

Preface of a Saint, or of Trinity Sunday

Common of a Monastic I

I O God, whose blessed Son became poor that we through his poverty might be rich: Deliver us, we pray thee, from an inordinate love of this world, that, inspired by the devotion of thy servant N., we may serve thee with singleness of heart, and attain to the riches of the age to come; through the same thy Son Jesus Christ our Lord, who liveth and reigneth with thee, in the unity of the Holy Spirit, one God, now and for ever. *Amen.*

II O God, whose blessed Son became poor that we through his poverty might be rich: Deliver us from an inordinate love of this world, that we, inspired by the devotion of your servant N., may serve you with singleness of heart, and attain to the riches of the age to come; through Jesus Christ our Lord, who lives and reigns with you, in the unity of the Holy Spirit, one God, now and for ever. *Amen.*

Psalm	Lessons
34	Song of Songs 8:6–7 Philippians 3:7–15 Luke 12:33–37 *or* Luke 9:57–62

Preface of a Saint

Common of a Monastic II

I O God, by whose grace thy servant *N.*, enkindled with the fire of thy love, became a burning and a shining light in thy Church: Grant that we also may be aflame with the spirit of love and discipline, and may ever walk before thee as children of light; through Jesus Christ our Lord, who with thee, in the unity of the Holy Spirit, liveth and reigneth, one God, now and for ever. *Amen.*

II O God, by whose grace your servant *N.*, kindled with the flame of your love, became a burning and a shining light in your Church: Grant that we also may be aflame with the spirit of love and discipline, and walk before you as children of light; through Jesus Christ our Lord, who lives and reigns with you, in the unity of the Holy Spirit, one God, now and for ever. *Amen.*

Psalm	Lessons
133	Acts 2:42–47a
or 34:1–8	2 Corinthians 6:1–10
or 119:161–168	Matthew 6:24–33

Preface of a Saint

Common of a Saint I

I O Almighty God, who hast compassed us about with so great a cloud of witnesses: Grant that we, encouraged by the good example of thy servant N., may persevere in running the race that is set before us, until at length, through thy mercy, we may with *him* attain to thine eternal joy; through Jesus Christ, the author and perfecter of our faith, who liveth and reigneth with thee and the Holy Spirit, one God, for ever and ever. *Amen.*

II Almighty God, you have surrounded us with a great cloud of witnesses: Grant that we, encouraged by the good example of your servant N., may persevere in running the race that is set before us, until at last we may with *him* attain to your eternal joy; through Jesus Christ, the pioneer and perfecter of our faith, who lives and reigns with you and the Holy Spirit, one God, for ever and ever. *Amen.*

Psalm	Lessons
15	Micah 6:6–8
	Hebrews 12:1–2
	Matthew 25:31–40

Preface of a Saint

Common of a Saint II

I O God, who hast brought us near to an innumerable company of angels and to the spirits of just men made perfect: Grant us during our earthly pilgrimage to abide in their fellowship, and in our heavenly country to become partakers of their joy; through Jesus Christ our Lord, who liveth and reigneth with thee and the Holy Spirit, one God, now and for ever. *Amen.*

II O God, you have brought us near to an innumerable company of angels, and to the spirits of just men made perfect: Grant us during our earthly pilgrimage to abide in their fellowship, and in our heavenly country to become partakers of their joy; through Jesus Christ our Lord, who lives and reigns with you and the Holy Spirit, one God, now and for ever. *Amen.*

Psalm	Lessons
34	Wisdom 3:1–9
or 34:15–22	Philippians 4:4–9
	Luke 6:17–23

Preface of a Saint

Common of a Saint III

I O Almighty God, who by thy Holy Spirit hast made us one with thy saints in heaven and on earth: Grant that in our earthly pilgrimage we may ever be supported by this fellowship of love and prayer, and may know ourselves to be surrounded by their witness to thy power and mercy. We ask this for the sake of Jesus Christ, in whom all our intercessions are acceptable through the Spirit, and who liveth and reigneth for ever and ever. *Amen.*

II Almighty God, by your Holy Spirit you have made us one with your saints in heaven and on earth: Grant that in our earthly pilgrimage we may always be supported by this fellowship of love and prayer, and know ourselves to be surrounded by their witness to your power and mercy. We ask this for the sake of Jesus Christ, in whom all our intercessions are acceptable through the Spirit, and who lives and reigns for ever and ever. *Amen.*

Psalm	Lessons
1	Sirach (Ecclesiasticus) 2:7–11 1 Corinthians 1:26–31 Matthew 25:1–13

Preface of a Saint

New Commons of Saints

Common of Artists, Writers, and Composers

I Eternal God, light of the world and Creator of all that is good and lovely: We bless thy name for inspiring [N. and] all those who, with images and music and words, hath filled us with desire and love for thee; through Jesus Christ our Savior, who with thee and the Holy Spirit liveth and reigneth, one God, for ever and ever. *Amen.*

II Eternal God, light of the world and Creator of all that is good and lovely: We bless your name for inspiring [N. and] all those who with images and music and words have filled us with desire and love for you; through Jesus Christ our Savior, who with you and the Holy Spirit lives and reigns, one God, for ever and ever. *Amen.*

Psalm	Lessons
90: 14–17	1 Chronicles 29:14b–19
	2 Corinthians 3:1–3
	John 21:15–17, 24–25

Preface of Artists, Writers, and Composers

I Because in the beauty of holiness thou hast called us to worship thee; and hast given faithful artists, writers, and composers to illumine our prayer from age to age.

II Because in the beauty of holiness you call us to worship you, and you have given faithful artists, writers, and composers to illumine our prayer from age to age.

Common of the Blessed Virgin Mary, Godbearer

Of the Blessed Virgin Mary, Godbearer I

I Almighty God, by thy saving grace thou didst call Mary of Nazareth to be the mother of thine only Son: inspire us by the same grace to follow her example of bearing God to the world. We pray through Jesus Christ her Son, our Savior. *Amen.*

II Almighty God, of your saving grace you called Mary of Nazareth to be the mother of your only begotten Son: Inspire us by the same grace to follow her example of bearing God to the world. We pray through Jesus Christ her Son, our Savior. *Amen.*

Of the Blessed Virgin Mary, Godbearer II

I Holy God, we magnify thy Name for calling the blessed Virgin Mary to bear thy Word of hope to the poor, the hungry, and those who have no voice: Give unto us thy grace and strength, that we might proclaim thy Good News in every age, with every tongue; through Jesus Christ our Savior, in the power of thy Holy Spirit. *Amen.*

II Holy God, we magnify your Name for calling the blessed Virgin Mary to bear your Word of hope to the poor, the hungry, and those who have no voice: Give us grace and strength to proclaim your Good News in every age, with every tongue; through Jesus Christ our Savior, in the power of your Holy Spirit. *Amen.*

Psalm	Lessons
34: 1–8	Isaiah 43:9–13, 19a 1 Corinthians 1:26–31 Luke 1:42–45

Preface of the Blessed Virgin Mary, Godbearer

I Because even as blessed Mary didst consent to become Godbearer for the world, thou hast called us to bear thy Word to all whom our lives touch.

II Because as blessed Mary consented to become Godbearer for the world, you call us to bear your Word to all whom our lives touch.

Common of Prophetic Witness in the Church

I   Gracious Father, we pray for thy holy Catholic Church. Fill it with all truth, in all truth with all peace. Where it is corrupt, purify it; where it is in error, direct it; where in anything it is amiss, reform it. Where it is right, strengthen it; where it is in want, provide for it; where it is divided, reunite it; for the sake of Jesus Christ thy Son our Savior, who with thee and the Holy Spirit liveth and reigneth, one God, now and for ever. *Amen.*

II   Gracious Father, we pray for your holy Catholic Church. Fill it with all truth, in all truth with all peace. Where it is corrupt, purify it; where it is in error, direct it; where in anything it is amiss, reform it. Where it is right, strengthen it; where it is in want, provide for it; where it is divided, reunite it; for the sake of Jesus Christ your Son our Savior, who with you and the Holy Spirit lives and reigns, one God, now and for ever. *Amen.*

Psalm	**Lessons**
12:1-7	Ezekiel 34:1-6,20-22
	Acts 22:30-23:10
	Matthew 21:12-16

Preface of Prophetic Witness in the Church

I   For thou dost cleanse and renew thy Church by the witness of thy saints, calling people in every age to holiness of life through the indwelling of thy Holy Spirit.

II   For you cleanse and renew your Church by the witness of your saints, calling people in every age to holiness of life through the indwelling of your Holy Spirit.

Common of Prophetic Witness in Society

I   Almighty God, whose prophets hath taught us righteousness in the care of thy poor: By the guidance of thy Holy Spirit, grant that we may do justice, love mercy, and walk humbly in thy sight; through Jesus Christ, our Judge and Redeemer, who liveth and reigneth, with thee and the same Spirit ever one God. *Amen.*

II   Almighty God, whose prophets taught us righteousness in the care of your poor: By the guidance of your Holy Spirit, grant that we may do justice, love mercy, and walk humbly in your sight; through Jesus Christ, our Judge and Redeemer, who lives and reigns with you and the same Spirit, one God, now and for ever. *Amen.*

Psalm	Lessons
2:1-2,10-12	Isaiah 55:11-56:1
	Acts 14:14-17,21-23
	Mark 4:21-29

Preface of Prophetic Witness in Society

I   Because in every age thou hast called brave souls to proclaim righteousness for the transformation of the world, that all may welcome the coming of thy holy reign.

II   Because in every age you have called brave souls to proclaim righteousness for the transformation of the world, that all may welcome the coming of your holy reign.

Common of Scientists and Environmentalists

I God of grace and glory, thou didst create and sustain the universe in majesty and beauty: We thank you for [N. and] all in whom thou hast planted the desire to know thy creation and to explore thy work and wisdom. Lead us, like them, to understand better the wonder and mystery of creation; through Christ thine eternal Word, through whom all things were made. *Amen.*

II God of grace and glory, you create and sustain the universe in majesty and beauty: We thank you for [N. and] all in whom you have planted the desire to know your creation and to explore your work and wisdom. Lead us, like them, to understand better the wonder and mystery of creation; through Christ your eternal Word, through whom all things were made. *Amen.*

Psalm	Lessons
34:8-14	Genesis 2:9-20
	2 Corinthians 13:1-6
	John 20:24-27

Preface of Scientists and Environmentalists

I Because thou dost inspire us to seek thy face in the wonders of thy creation, and revealest thy work, that thy people may rejoice in thy many gifts.

II Because you inspire us to seek your face in the wonders of your creation, and you reveal your work, so that your people may rejoice in your many gifts.

4. Various Occasions

Introduction

The original design for the 1979 Book of Common Prayer included a set of eucharistic propers for Special Occasions. Now referred to as propers for Various Occasions, they are the direct heirs of medieval votive propers and fill the need for special celebrations for either intercessory or devotional purposes. They reflect concerns or celebrations that are either particularly pertinent to the ongoing life of the Church or are recurrent enough in the life of the Church to be necessary.

Since these propers were composed for the 1979 Prayer Book, new occasions and concerns have been identified that connect to modern church life. This book continues the use of propers introduced in 2009 in *Holy Women, Holy Men*.

These propers for Various Occasions may be used on any weekday or on a Sunday outside of the principal service, "subject to the rules of precedence governing Principal Feasts, Sundays, and Holy Days" (BCP, 15–17) and provided "that none of Propers appointed for Various Occasions is used as a substitute for, or in addition to, the Proper appointed for the Principal Feasts" (BCP, 18).

During Lent, the propers For the Ministry I, II, and III may be used on the traditional Ember Days (Wednesday, Friday, and Saturday following the First Sunday in Lent). Other propers for Various Occasions are not ordinarily used during the season of Lent in order to preserve the distinctive character of the season.

In the Sarum liturgies before the time of the Reformation, certain votive propers were used regularly in a weekly cycle. The first seven propers of our Prayer Book recall this sequence, substituting the proper "For All Baptized Christians" in the position historically occupied by a votive in honor of the Blessed Virgin Mary.

The Daily Office and the Propers for Various Occasions

The collects for Various Occasions are appropriate for use in the time designated for "authorized intercessions and thanksgivings" following the prayer for mission in the Daily Office. The scriptural readings for Various Occasions are not intended to displace the regular cycle of readings appointed for the Daily Office.

Various Occasions

For optional use, when desired, subject to the rules set forth in the Calendar of the church year.

1. Of the Holy Trinity

I   Almighty God, who hast revealed to thy Church thine eternal Being of glorious majesty and perfect love as one God in Trinity of Persons: Give us grace to continue steadfast in the confession of this faith, and constant in our worship of thee, Father, Son, and Holy Spirit; who livest and reignest, one God, now and for ever. *Amen.*

II   Almighty God, you have revealed to your Church your eternal Being of glorious majesty and perfect love as one God in Trinity of Persons: Give us grace to continue steadfast in the confession of this faith, and constant in our worship of you, Father, Son, and Holy Spirit; for you live and reign, one God, now and for ever. *Amen.*

Psalm	**Lessons**
29	Exodus 3:11-15
	Romans 11:33-36
	Matthew 28:18-20

Preface of Trinity Sunday

2. Of the Holy Spirit

I   Almighty and most merciful God, grant, we beseech thee, that by the indwelling of thy Holy Spirit we may be enlightened and strengthened for thy service; through Jesus Christ our Lord, who liveth and reigneth with thee, in the unity of the same Spirit ever, one God, world without end. *Amen.*

II   Almighty and most merciful God, grant that by the indwelling of your Holy Spirit we may be enlightened and strengthened for your service; through Jesus Christ our Lord, who lives and reigns with you, in the unity of the Holy Spirit, one God, now and for ever. *Amen.*

Psalm	**Lessons**
139:1-17	Isaiah 61:1-3
or 139:1-9	1 Corinthians 12:4-14
	Luke 11:9-13

Preface of Pentecost

3. Of the Holy Angels

I O everlasting God, who hast ordained and constituted the ministries of angels and men in a wonderful order: Mercifully grant that, as thy holy angels always serve and worship thee in heaven, so by thy appointment they may help and defend us on earth; through Jesus Christ our Lord, who liveth and reigneth with thee and the Holy Spirit, one God, for ever and ever. *Amen.*

II Everlasting God, you have ordained and constituted in a wonderful order the ministries of angels and mortals: Mercifully grant that, as your holy angels always serve and worship you in heaven, so by your appointment they may help and defend us here on earth; through Jesus Christ our Lord, who lives and reigns with you and the Holy Spirit, one God, for ever and ever. *Amen.*

Psalm	**Lessons**
148	Daniel 7:9-10a
or 103:19-22	*or* 2 Kings 6:8-17
	Revelation 5:11-14
	John 1:47-51

Preface of Trinity Sunday

4. Of the Incarnation

I O God, who didst wonderfully create, and yet more wonderfully restore, the dignity of human nature: Grant that we may share the divine life of him who humbled himself to share our humanity, thy Son Jesus Christ; who liveth and reigneth with thee, in the unity of the Holy Spirit, one God, for ever and ever. *Amen.*

II O God, who wonderfully created, and yet more wonderfully restored, the dignity of human nature: Grant that we may share the divine life of him who humbled himself to share our humanity, your Son Jesus Christ; who lives and reigns with you, in the unity of the Holy Spirit, one God, for ever and ever. *Amen.*

Psalm	Lessons
111	Isaiah 11:1-10
or 132:11-19	*or* Genesis 17:1-8
	1 John 4:1-11
	or 1 Timothy 3:14-16
	Luke 1:26-33(34-38)
	or Luke 11:27-28

Preface of the Epiphany

5. Of the Holy Eucharist

Especially suitable for Thursdays

I God our Father, whose Son our Lord Jesus Christ in a wonderful Sacrament hath left unto us a memorial of his passion: Grant us so to venerate the sacred mysteries of his Body and Blood, that we may ever perceive within ourselves the fruit of his redemption; who liveth and reigneth with thee and the Holy Spirit, one God, for ever and ever. *Amen.*

II God our Father, whose Son our Lord Jesus Christ in a wonderful Sacrament has left us a memorial of his passion: Grant us so to venerate the sacred mysteries of his Body and Blood, that we may ever perceive within ourselves the fruit of his redemption; who lives and reigns with you and the Holy Spirit, one God, for ever and ever. *Amen.*

Psalm	Lessons
34	Deuteronomy 8:2-3
or 116:10-17	Revelation 19:1-2a,4-9
	or 1 Corinthians 10:1-4,16-17
	or 1 Corinthians 11:23-29
	John 6:47-58

Preface of the Epiphany

6. Of the Holy Cross

Especially suitable for Fridays

I   Almighty God, whose beloved Son willingly endured the agony and shame of the cross for our redemption: Give us courage, we beseech thee, to take up our cross and follow him; who liveth and reigneth with thee and the Holy Spirit, one God, now and for ever. *Amen.*

II Almighty God, whose beloved Son willingly endured the agony and shame of the cross for our redemption: Give us courage to take up our cross and follow him; who lives and reigns with you and the Holy Spirit, one God, now and for ever. *Amen.*

Psalm	Lessons
40:1-11	Isaiah 52:13-15; 53:10-12
or 40:5-11	1 Corinthians 1:18-24
	John 12:23-33

Preface of Holy Week

7. For All Baptized Christians

Especially suitable for Saturdays

I   Grant, O Lord God, to all who have been baptized into the death and resurrection of thy Son Jesus Christ, that, as we have put away the old life of sin, so we may be renewed in the spirit of our minds, and live in righteousness and true holiness; through the same Jesus Christ our Lord, who liveth and reigneth with thee, in the unity of the Holy Spirit, one God, now and for ever. *Amen.*

II   Grant, Lord God, to all who have been baptized into the death and resurrection of your Son Jesus Christ, that, as we have put away the old life of sin, so we may be renewed in the spirit of our minds, and live in righteousness and true holiness; through Jesus Christ our Lord, who lives and reigns with you, in the unity of the Holy Spirit, one God, now and for ever. *Amen.*

Psalm	Lessons
16:5-11	Jeremiah 17:7-8 *or* Ezekiel 36:24-28 Romans 6:3-11 Mark 10:35-45

Preface of Baptism

8. For the Departed

For the Departed I

I O eternal Lord God, who holdest all souls in life: Give, we beseech thee, to thy whole Church in paradise and on earth thy light and thy peace; and grant that we, following the good examples of those who have served thee here and are now at rest, may at the last enter with them into thine unending joy; through Jesus Christ our Lord, who liveth and reigneth with thee, in the unity of the Holy Spirit, one God, now and for ever. *Amen.*

II Eternal Lord God, you hold all souls in life: Give to your whole Church in paradise and on earth your light and your peace; and grant that we, following the good examples of those who have served you here and are now at rest, may at the last enter with them into your unending joy; through Jesus Christ our Lord, who lives and reigns with you, in the unity of the Holy Spirit, one God, now and for ever. *Amen.*

For the Departed II

I Almighty God, we remember this day before thee thy faithful servant N.; and we pray that, having opened to *him* the gates of larger life, thou wilt receive *him* more and more into thy joyful service, that, with all who have faithfully served thee in the past, *he* may share in the eternal victory of Jesus Christ our Lord; who liveth and reigneth with thee, in the unity of the Holy Spirit, one God, for ever and ever. *Amen.*

II Almighty God, we remember before you today your faithful servant N.; and we pray that, having opened to *him* the gates of larger life, you will receive *him* more and more into your joyful service, that, with all who have faithfully served you in the past, *he* may share in the eternal victory of Jesus Christ our Lord; who lives and reigns with you, in the unity of the Holy Spirit, one God, for ever and ever. *Amen.*

Any of the Collects appointed for use at the Burial of the Dead may be used instead.

Psalm	Lessons
116	Isaiah 25: 6-9
or 103:13-22	*or* Wisdom 3:1-9
or 130	1 Corinthians 15:50-58
	John 5:24-27
	or John 6:37-40
	or John 11:21-27

Any of the Psalms and Lessons appointed at the Burial of the Dead may be used instead.

For the Prayers of the People, one of the forms appointed for the Burial of the Dead may be used.

Preface of the Commemoration of the Dead

The postcommunion prayer on page 482 or 498 of the Book of Common Prayer may be used.

9. Of the Reign of Christ

I   Almighty and everlasting God, whose will it is to restore all things in thy well-beloved Son, the King of kings and Lord of lords: Mercifully grant that the peoples of the earth, divided and enslaved by sin, may be freed and brought together under his most gracious rule; who liveth and reigneth with thee and the Holy Spirit, one God, now and for ever. *Amen.*

II   Almighty and everlasting God, whose will it is to restore all things in your well-beloved Son, the King of kings and Lord of lords: Mercifully grant that the peoples of the earth, divided and enslaved by sin, may be freed and brought together under his most gracious rule; who lives and reigns with you and the Holy Spirit, one God, now and for ever. *Amen.*

Psalm	**Lessons**
93	Daniel 7:9-14
or Canticle 18	Colossians 1:11-20
	John 18:33-37

Any of the Psalms and Lessons appointed in Proper 29 may be used instead.

Preface of the Ascension, or of Baptism

10. At Baptism

I   Almighty God, who by our baptism into the death and resurrection of thy Son Jesus Christ dost turn us from the old life of sin: Grant that we, being reborn to new life in him, may live in righteousness and holiness all our days; through the same thy Son Jesus Christ our Lord, who liveth and reigneth with thee and the Holy Spirit, one God, now and for ever. *Amen.*

II   Almighty God, by our baptism into the death and resurrection of your Son Jesus Christ, you turn us from the old life of sin: Grant that we, being reborn to new life in him, may live in righteousness and holiness all our days; through Jesus Christ our Lord, who lives and reigns with you and the Holy Spirit, one God, now and for ever. *Amen.*

Psalm	Lessons
15	Ezekiel 36:24-28*
or 23	Romans 6:3-5
or 27	*or* Romans 8:14-17
or 42:1-7	*or* 2 Corinthians 5:17-20
or 84	Mark 1:9-11
or Canticle 9	*or* Mark 10:13-16
	or John 3:1-6

*Any of the other Old Testament Lessons for the Easter Vigil may be substituted.

Preface of Baptism

11. At Confirmation

I Grant, Almighty God, that we, who have been redeemed from the old life of sin by our baptism into the death and resurrection of thy Son Jesus Christ, may be renewed in thy Holy Spirit, and live in righteousness and true holiness; through the same Jesus Christ our Lord, who liveth and reigneth with thee and the same Spirit, one God, now and for ever. *Amen.*

II Grant, Almighty God, that we, who have been redeemed from the old life of sin by our baptism into the death and resurrection of your Son Jesus Christ, may be renewed in your Holy Spirit, and live in righteousness and true holiness; through Jesus Christ our Lord, who lives and reigns with you and the Holy Spirit, one God, now and for ever. *Amen.*

Psalm	**Lessons**
1	Isaiah 61:1-9
or 139:1-9	*or* Jeremiah 31:31-34
	or Ezekiel 37:1-10
	Romans 8:18-27
	or Romans 12:1-8
	or Galatians 5:16-25
	or Ephesians 4:7,11-16
	Matthew 5:1-12
	or Matthew 16:24-27
	or Luke 4:16-22
	or John 14:15-21

Preface of Baptism, or of Pentecost

12. On the Anniversary of the Dedication of a Church

I O Almighty God, to whose glory we celebrate the dedication of this house of prayer: We give thee thanks for the fellowship of those who have worshiped in this place; and we pray that all who seek thee here may find thee, and be filled with thy joy and peace; through Jesus Christ our Lord, who liveth and reigneth with thee, in the unity of the Holy Spirit, one God, now and for ever. *Amen.*

II Almighty God, to whose glory we celebrate the dedication of this house of prayer: We give you thanks for the fellowship of those who have worshiped in this place, and we pray that all who seek you here may find you, and be filled with your joy and peace; through Jesus Christ our Lord, who lives and reigns with you, in the unity of the Holy Spirit, one God, now and for ever. *Amen.*

Psalm	Lessons
84	1 Kings 8:22-30
or 84:1-6	*or* Genesis 28:10-17
	1 Peter 2:1-5,9-10
	Matthew 21:12-16

The Litany of Thanksgiving for a Church, page 578 of the Book of Common Prayer, may be used for the Prayers of the People.

Preface of the Dedication of a Church

13. For a Church Convention

I Almighty and everlasting Father, who hast given the Holy Spirit to abide with us for ever: Bless, we beseech thee, with his grace and presence, the bishops and the other clergy and the laity here (or now, or soon to be) assembled in thy Name, that thy Church, being preserved in true faith and godly discipline, may fulfill all the mind of him who loved it and gave himself for it, thy Son Jesus Christ our Savior; who liveth and reigneth with thee, in the unity of the same Spirit, one God, now and for ever. *Amen.*

II Almighty and everlasting Father, you have given the Holy Spirit to abide with us for ever: Bless, we pray, with his grace and presence, the bishops and the other clergy and the laity here (or now, or soon to be) assembled in your Name, that your Church, being preserved in true faith and godly discipline, may fulfill all the mind of him who loved it and gave himself for it, your Son Jesus Christ our Savior; who lives and reigns with you, in the unity of the Holy Spirit, one God, now and for ever. *Amen.*

Psalm	Lessons
19:7-14	Isaiah 55:1-13
	2 Corinthians 4:1-10
	John 15:1-11

Preface of Pentecost, or of the Season

14. For the Unity of the Church

I Almighty Father, whose blessed Son before his passion prayed for his disciples that they might be one, even as thou and he are one: Grant that thy Church, being bound together in love and obedience to thee, may be united in one body by the one Spirit, that the world may believe in him whom thou didst send, the same thy Son Jesus Christ our Lord; who liveth and reigneth with thee, in the unity of the same Spirit, one God, now and for ever. *Amen.*

II Almighty Father, whose blessed Son before his passion prayed for his disciples that they might be one, as you and he are one: Grant that your Church, being bound together in love and obedience to you, may be united in one body by the one Spirit, that the world may believe in him whom you have sent, your Son Jesus Christ our Lord; who lives and reigns with you, in the unity of the Holy Spirit, one God, now and for ever. *Amen.*

Psalm	Lessons
122	Isaiah 35:1-10
	Ephesians 4:1-6
	John 17:6a,15-23

Preface of Baptism, or of Trinity Sunday

15. For the Ministry (Ember Days)

For use on the traditional days or at other times

I. For those to be ordained

I   Almighty God, the giver of all good gifts, who of thy divine providence hast appointed various orders in thy Church: Give thy grace, we humbly beseech thee, to all who are [now] called to any office and ministry for thy people; and so fill them with the truth of thy doctrine and clothe them with holiness of life, that they may faithfully serve before thee, to the glory of thy great Name and for the benefit of thy holy Church; through Jesus Christ our Lord, who liveth and reigneth with thee, in the unity of the Holy Spirit, one God, now and for ever. *Amen.*

II   Almighty God, the giver of all good gifts, in your divine providence you have appointed various orders in your Church: Give your grace, we humbly pray, to all who are [now] called to any office and ministry for your people; and so fill them with the truth of your doctrine and clothe them with holiness of life, that they may faithfully serve before you, to the glory of your great Name and for the benefit of your holy Church; through Jesus Christ our Lord, who lives and reigns with you, in the unity of the Holy Spirit, one God, now and for ever. *Amen.*

Psalm	Lessons
99	Numbers 11:16-17,24-29
or 27:1-9	1 Corinthians 3:5-11
	John 4:31-38

Preface of Apostles

II. For the choice of fit persons for the ministry

I O God, who didst lead thy holy apostles to ordain ministers in every place: Grant that thy Church, under the guidance of the Holy Spirit, may choose suitable persons for the ministry of Word and Sacrament, and may uphold them in their work for the extension of thy kingdom; through him who is the Shepherd and Bishop of our souls, Jesus Christ our Lord, who liveth and reigneth with thee and the same Spirit, one God, for ever and ever. *Amen.*

II O God, you led your holy apostles to ordain ministers in every place: Grant that your Church, under the guidance of the Holy Spirit, may choose suitable persons for the ministry of Word and Sacrament, and may uphold them in their work for the extension of your kingdom; through him who is the Shepherd and Bishop of our souls, Jesus Christ our Lord, who lives and reigns with you and the Holy Spirit, one God, for ever and ever. *Amen.*

Psalm	**Lessons**
63:1-8	1 Samuel 3:1-10
	Ephesians 4:11-16
	Matthew 9:35-38

Preface of the Season

III. For all Christians in their vocation

I Almighty and everlasting God, by whose Spirit the whole body of thy faithful people is governed and sanctified: Receive our supplications and prayers, which we offer before thee for all members of thy holy Church, that in their vocation and ministry they may truly and godly serve thee; through our Lord and Savior Jesus Christ, who liveth and reigneth with thee, in the unity of the same Spirit, one God, now and for ever. *Amen.*

II Almighty and everlasting God, by whose Spirit the whole body of your faithful people is governed and sanctified: Receive our supplications and prayers, which we offer before you for all members of your holy Church, that in their vocation and ministry they may truly and devoutly serve you; through our Lord and Savior Jesus Christ, who lives and reigns with you, in the unity of the Holy Spirit, one God, now and for ever. *Amen.*

Psalm	**Lessons**
15	Exodus 19:3-8
	1 Peter 4:7-11
	Matthew 16:24-27

Preface of Baptism, or of the Season

16. For the Mission of the Church

For the Mission of the Church I

I O God, who hast made of one blood all the peoples of the earth, and didst send thy blessed Son to preach peace to those who are far off and to those who are near: Grant that people everywhere may seek after thee and find thee, bring the nations into thy fold, pour out thy Spirit upon all flesh, and hasten the coming of thy kingdom; through the same thy Son Jesus Christ our Lord, who liveth and reigneth with thee and the same Spirit, one God, now and for ever. *Amen.*

II O God, you have made of one blood all the peoples of the earth, and sent your blessed Son to preach peace to those who are far off and to those who are near: Grant that people everywhere may seek after you and find you, bring the nations into your fold, pour out your Spirit upon all flesh, and hasten the coming of your kingdom; through Jesus Christ our Lord, who lives and reigns with you and the Holy Spirit, one God, now and for ever. *Amen.*

Psalm	Lessons
96	Isaiah 2:2-4
or 96:1-7	Ephesians 2:13-22
	Luke 10:1-9

Preface of the Season, or of Pentecost

For the Mission of the Church II

I   O God of all the nations of the earth: Remember the multitudes who have been created in thine image but have not known the redeeming work of our Savior Jesus Christ and grant that, by the prayers and labors of thy holy Church, they may be brought to know and worship thee as thou hast been revealed in thy Son; who liveth and reigneth with thee and the Holy Spirit, one God, for ever and ever. *Amen.*

II   O God of all the nations of the earth: Remember the multitudes who have been created in your image but have not known the redeeming work of our Savior Jesus Christ; and grant that, by the prayers and labors of your holy Church, they may be brought to know and worship you as you have been revealed in your Son; who lives and reigns with you and the Holy Spirit, one God, for ever and ever. *Amen.*

Psalm	Lessons
67	Isaiah 49:5-13
	Ephesians 3:1-12
	Matthew 28:16-20

Preface of the Season, or of Pentecost

17. For the Nation

I   Lord God Almighty, who hast made all peoples of the earth for thy glory, to serve thee in freedom and peace: Grant to the people of our country a zeal for justice and the strength of forbearance, that we may use our liberty in accordance with thy gracious will; through Jesus Christ our Lord, who liveth and reigneth with thee and the Holy Spirit, one God, for ever and ever. *Amen.*

II Lord God Almighty, you have made all the peoples of the earth for your glory, to serve you in freedom and in peace: Give to the people of our country a zeal for justice and the strength of forbearance, that we may use our liberty in accordance with your gracious will; through Jesus Christ our Lord, who lives and reigns with you and the Holy Spirit, one God, for ever and ever. *Amen.*

The Collect for Independence Day may be used instead.

Psalm	Lessons
47	Isaiah 26:1-8
	Romans 13:1-10
	Mark 12:13-17

The Psalm and any of the Lessons appointed for Independence Day may be used instead.

Preface of Trinity Sunday

18. For Peace

I O Almighty God, kindle, we beseech thee, in every heart the true love of peace, and guide with thy wisdom those who take counsel for the nations of the earth, that in tranquility thy dominion may increase till the earth is filled with the knowledge of thy love; through Jesus Christ our Lord, who liveth and reigneth with thee, in the unity of the Holy Spirit, one God, now and for ever. *Amen.*

II Almighty God, kindle, we pray, in every heart the true love of peace, and guide with your wisdom those who take counsel for the nations of the earth, that in tranquility your dominion may increase until the earth is filled with the knowledge of your love; through Jesus Christ our Lord, who lives and reigns with you, in the unity of the Holy Spirit, one God, now and for ever. *Amen.*

Psalm	Lessons
85:7-13	Micah 4:1-5
	Ephesians 2:13-18
	or Colossians 3:12-15
	John 16:23-33
	or Matthew 5:43-48

Preface of the Season

19. For Rogation Days

For use on the traditional days or at other times

I. *For fruitful seasons*

I Almighty God, Lord of heaven and earth: We humbly pray that thy gracious providence may give and preserve to our use the harvests of the land and of the seas, and may prosper all who labor to gather them, that we, who constantly receive good things from thy hand, may always give thee thanks; through Jesus Christ our Lord, who liveth and reigneth with thee and the Holy Spirit, one God, for ever and ever. *Amen.*

II Almighty God, Lord of heaven and earth: We humbly pray that your gracious providence may give and preserve to our use the harvests of the land and of the seas, and may prosper all who labor to gather them, that we, who are constantly receiving good things from your hand, may always give you thanks; through Jesus Christ our Lord, who lives and reigns with you and the Holy Spirit, one God, for ever and ever. *Amen.*

Psalm	Lessons
147	Deuteronomy 11:10-15
or 147:1-13	*or* Ezekiel 47:6-12
	or Jeremiah 14:1-9
	Romans 8:18-25
	Mark 4:26-32

Preface of the Season

II. For commerce and industry

I   Almighty God, whose Son Jesus Christ in his earthly life shared our toil and hallowed our labor: Be present with thy people where they work; make those who carry on the industries and commerce of this land responsive to thy will; and give to us all a pride in what we do, and a just return for our labor; through Jesus Christ our Lord, who liveth and reigneth with thee, in the unity of the Holy Spirit, one God, now and for ever. *Amen.*

II   Almighty God, whose Son Jesus Christ in his earthly life shared our toil and hallowed our labor: Be present with your people where they work; make those who carry on the industries and commerce of this land responsive to your will; and give to us all a pride in what we do, and a just return for our labor; through Jesus Christ our Lord, who lives and reigns with you, in the unity of the Holy Spirit, one God, now and for ever. *Amen.*

Psalm	Lessons
107:1-9	Ecclesiasticus 38:27-32
	1 Corinthians 3:10-14
	Matthew 6:19-24

Preface of the Season

III. For stewardship of creation

I   O merciful Creator, whose hand is open wide to satisfy the needs of every living creature: Make us, we beseech thee, ever thankful for thy loving providence; and grant that we, remembering the account that we must one day give, may be faithful stewards of thy bounty; through Jesus Christ our Lord, who with thee and the Holy Spirit liveth and reigneth, one God, for ever and ever. *Amen.*

II   O merciful Creator, your hand is open wide to satisfy the needs of every living creature: Make us always thankful for your loving providence; and grant that we, remembering the account that we must one day give, may be faithful stewards of your good gifts; through Jesus Christ our Lord, who with you and the Holy Spirit lives and reigns, one God, for ever and ever. *Amen.*

Psalm	**Lessons**
104:25-37	Job 38:1-11,16-18
or 104:1,13-15,	1 Timothy 6:7-10,17-19
25-32	Luke 12:13-21

Preface of the Season

20. For the Sick

I   Heavenly Father, giver of life and health: Comfort and relieve thy sick servants, and give thy power of healing to those who minister to their needs, that those (*or N., or NN.*) for whom our prayers are offered may be strengthened in *their* weakness and have confidence in thy loving care; through Jesus Christ our Lord, who liveth and reigneth with thee and the Holy Spirit, one God, now and for ever. *Amen.*

II Heavenly Father, giver of life and health: Comfort and relieve your sick servants, and give your power of healing to those who minister to their needs, that those (*or N., or NN.*) for whom our prayers are offered may be strengthened in *their* weakness and have confidence in your loving care; through Jesus Christ our Lord, who lives and reigns with you and the Holy Spirit, one God, now and for ever. *Amen.*

Psalm	**Lessons**
13	2 Kings 20:1-5
or 86:1-7	James 5:13-16
	Mark 2:1-12

Any of the Psalms and Lessons appointed at the Ministration to the Sick (BCP, 453-54) may be used instead.

Preface of the Season

The postcommunion prayer on page 457 of the Book of Common Prayer may be used.

21. For Social Justice

I   Almighty God, who hast created us in thine own image: Grant us grace fearlessly to contend against evil and to make no peace with oppression; and, that we may reverently use our freedom, help us to employ it in the maintenance of justice in our communities and among the nations, to the glory of thy holy Name; through Jesus Christ our Lord, who liveth and reigneth with thee and the Holy Spirit, one God, now and for ever. *Amen.*

II Almighty God, who created us in your own image: Grant us grace fearlessly to contend against evil and to make no peace with oppression; and, that we may reverently use our freedom, help us to employ it in the maintenance of justice in our communities and among the nations, to the glory of your holy Name; through Jesus Christ our Lord, who lives and reigns with you and the Holy Spirit, one God, now and for ever. *Amen.*

Psalm	**Lessons**
72	Isaiah 42:1-7
or 72:1-4,12-14	James 2:5-9,12-17
	Matthew 10:32-42

Preface of the Season

22. For Social Service

I O Lord our heavenly Father, whose blessed Son came not to be ministered unto but to minister: Bless, we beseech thee, all who, following in his steps, give themselves to the service of others; that with wisdom, patience, and courage, they may minister in his name to the suffering, the friendless, and the needy; for the love of him who laid down his life for us, the same thy Son our Savior Jesus Christ, who liveth and reigneth with thee and the Holy Spirit, one God, for ever and ever. *Amen.*

II Heavenly Father, whose blessed Son came not to be served but to serve: Bless all who, following in his steps, give themselves to the service of others; that with wisdom, patience, and courage, they may minister in his Name to the suffering, the friendless, and the needy; for the love of him who laid down his life for us, your Son our Savior Jesus Christ, who lives and reigns with you and the Holy Spirit, one God, for ever and ever. *Amen.*

Psalm	Lessons
146	Zechariah 8:3-12,16-17
or 22:22-27	1 Peter 4:7-11
	Mark 10:42-52

Preface of the Season

23. For Education

I Almighty God, the fountain of all wisdom: Enlighten by thy Holy Spirit those who teach and those who learn, that, rejoicing in the knowledge of thy truth, they may worship thee and serve thee from generation to generation; through Jesus Christ our Lord, who liveth and reigneth with thee and the same Spirit, one God, for ever and ever. *Amen.*

II Almighty God, the fountain of all wisdom: Enlighten by your Holy Spirit those who teach and those who learn, that, rejoicing in the knowledge of your truth, they may worship you and serve you from generation to generation; through Jesus Christ our Lord, who lives and reigns with you and the Holy Spirit, one God, for ever and ever. *Amen.*

Psalm	**Lessons**
78:1-7	Deuteronomy 6:4-9,20-25
	2 Timothy 3:14—4:5
	Matthew 11:25-30

Preface of the Season

24. For Vocation in Daily Work

I   Almighty God our heavenly Father, who declarest thy glory and showest forth thy handiwork in the heavens and in the earth: Deliver us, we beseech thee, in our several occupations from the service of self alone, that we may do the work which thou givest us to do, in truth and beauty and for the common good; for the sake of him who came among us as one that serveth, thy Son Jesus Christ our Lord, who liveth and reigneth with thee and the Holy Spirit, one God, for ever and ever. *Amen.*

II Almighty God our heavenly Father, you declare your glory and show forth your handiwork in the heavens and in the earth: Deliver us in our various occupations from the service of self alone, that we may do the work you give us to do in truth and beauty and for the common good; for the sake of him who came among us as one who serves, your Son Jesus Christ our Lord, who lives and reigns with you and the Holy Spirit, one God, for ever and ever. *Amen.*

Psalm	Lessons
8	Ecclesiastes 3:1,9-13
	1 Peter 2:11-17
	Matthew 6:19-24

Preface of the Season

25. For Labor Day

I Almighty God, who hast so linked our lives one with another that all we do affects, for good or ill, all other lives: So guide us in the work we do, that we may do it not for self alone, but for the common good; and, as we seek a proper return for our own labor, make us mindful of the rightful aspirations of other workers, and arouse our concern for those who are out of work; through Jesus Christ our Lord, who liveth and reigneth with thee and the Holy Spirit, one God, for ever and ever. *Amen.*

II Almighty God, you have so linked our lives one with another that all we do affects, for good or ill, all other lives: So guide us in the work we do, that we may do it not for self alone, but for the common good; and, as we seek a proper return for our own labor, make us mindful of the rightful aspirations of other workers, and arouse our concern for those who are out of work; through Jesus Christ our Lord, who lives and reigns with you and the Holy Spirit, one God, for ever and ever. *Amen.*

Psalm	**Lessons**
107:1-9	Ecclesiasticus 38:27-32
or 90:1-2,16-17	1 Corinthians 3:10-14
	Matthew 6:19-24

Preface of the Season

New Propers for Various Occasions

Care of God's Creation

I   Bountiful Creator, thou openest thy hand to satisfy the needs of every living creature: Make us continually thankful for thy loving providence, and grant that we, remembering the account we must one day give, may be faithful stewards of thine abundance, for the benefit of the whole creation; through Jesus Christ our Lord, through whom all things are made, who liveth and reigneth with thee and the Holy Spirit, one God, for ever and ever. *Amen.*

II   Bountiful Creator, you open your hand to satisfy the needs of every living creature: Make us always thankful for your loving providence, and grant that we, remembering the account we must one day give, may be faithful stewards of your abundance, for the benefit of the whole creation; through Jesus Christ our Lord, through whom all things were made, and who lives and reigns with you and the Holy Spirit, one God, for ever and ever. *Amen.*

Psalm	Lessons
145:1-7,22	1 Kings 4:29-30,33-34
	Acts 17:24-31
	John 1:1-5,9-14

Preface

I   For thou hast brought us into being and called us to care for the earth.

II   Because you have brought us into being and called us to care for the earth.

Goodness of God's Creation

I God of creation, we thank thee for all that thou hast made and called good: Grant that we may rightly serve and conserve the earth, and live at peace with all thy creatures; through Jesus Christ, the firstborn of all creation, in whom thou art reconciling the whole world unto thyself. *Amen.*

II God of creation, we thank you for all that you have made and called good: Grant that we may rightly serve and conserve the earth, and live at peace with all your creatures; through Jesus Christ, the firstborn of all creation, in whom you are reconciling the whole world to yourself. *Amen.*

Psalm	Lessons
104: 24-31	Job 14:7-9
	Romans 1:20-23
	Mark 16:14-15

Preface

I Because in thy loving kindness, thou hast brought the whole creation into being and blessed its goodness.

II Instead of a Preface, Prayer D is recommended for use with this Proper.

On the Occasion of a Disaster

I Compassionate God, whose Son Jesus wept at the grave of his friend Lazarus: Draw near to us in this time of sorrow and anguish, comfort those who mourn, strengthen those who are weary, encourage those in despair, and lead us all to fullness of life; through the same Jesus Christ, our Savior and Redeemer, who liveth and reigneth with thee, in the unity of the Holy Spirit, God for ever and ever. *Amen.*

II Compassionate God, whose Son Jesus wept at the grave of his friend Lazarus: Draw near to us in this time of sorrow and anguish, comfort those who mourn, strengthen those who are weary, encourage those in despair, and lead us all to fullness of life; through the same Jesus Christ, our Savior and Redeemer, who lives and reigns with you, in the unity of the Holy Spirit, God for ever and ever. *Amen.*

Psalm	**Lessons**
60:1-5	Job 14:7-13
or 130	*or* Jeremiah 31:15-20
or 80:1-7	Romans 8:35-38
or 23	*or* Revelation 21:1-7
	or Romans 8:18-25
	Luke 6:20-26
	or Mark 13:14-27

Preface of God the Son
or *Preface of the Commemoration of the Dead*

On the Anniversary of a Disaster

I God of steadfast love, who didst lead thy people through the wilderness: Be with us as we remember [and grieve]. By thy grace, lead us, we pray, in the path of new life, in the company of thy saints and angels; through Jesus Christ, the Savior and Redeemer of the world. *Amen.*

II God of steadfast love, who led your people through the wilderness: Be with us as we remember [and grieve]. By your grace, lead us in the path of new life, in the company of your saints and angels; through Jesus Christ, the Savior and Redeemer of the world. *Amen.*

Psalm	**Lessons**
60:1-5	Job 14:7-13
or 130	*or* Jeremiah 31:15-20
or 80:1-7	Romans 8:35-38
or 23	*or* Revelation 21:1-7
	or Romans 8:18-25
	Luke 6:20-26
	or Mark 13:14-27

Preface of God the Son
or *Preface of the Commemoration of the Dead*

Reconciliation and Forgiveness

I   God of compassion, thou hast reconciled us in Jesus Christ who is our peace: Enable us to live as Jesus lived, breaking down walls of hostility and healing enmity. Give us grace to make peace with those from whom we are divided, that, forgiven and forgiving, we may ever be one in Christ; who with thee and the Holy Spirit reigneth for ever, one holy and undivided Trinity. *Amen.*

II God of compassion, you have reconciled us in Jesus Christ who is our peace: Enable us to live as Jesus lived, breaking down walls of hostility and healing enmity. Give us grace to make peace with those from whom we are divided, that, forgiven and forgiving, we may ever be one in Christ; who with you and the Holy Spirit reigns for ever, one holy and undivided Trinity. *Amen.*

Psalm	Lessons
51:1-17	Genesis 8:12-17,20-22
	Hebrews 4:12-16
	Luke 23:32-43

Preface

I   Because by the cross of our Lord Jesus Christ thou hast reconciled all things to thyself, not counting our sins against us and renewing our hearts to forgive as we have been forgiven.

II Because by the cross of our Lord Jesus Christ you have reconciled all things to yourself, not counting our sins against us and renewing our hearts to forgive as we have been forgiven.

Space Exploration

I   Creator of the universe, whose dominion extends through the immensity of space: guide and guard those who seek to fathom its mysteries [especially *N.N*]. Save us from arrogance lest we forget that our achievements are grounded in thee, and, by the grace of thy Holy Spirit, protect our travels beyond the reaches of earth, that we may glory ever more in the wonder of thy creation: through Jesus Christ, thy Word, by whom all things came to be, who with thee and the Holy Spirit liveth and reigneth, one God, for ever and ever. *Amen.*

II Creator of the universe, your dominion extends through the immensity of space: guide and guard those who seek to fathom its mysteries [especially *N.N.*]. Save us from arrogance lest we forget that our achievements are grounded in you, and, by the grace of your Holy Spirit, protect our travels beyond the reaches of earth, that we may glory ever more in the wonder of your creation: through Jesus Christ, your Word, by whom all things came to be, who with you and the Holy Spirit lives and reigns, one God, for ever and ever. *Amen.*

Psalm	**Lessons**
19:1-6	Job 38: 4-12,16-18
or Canticle 12	Revelation 1:7-8,12-16
	John 15:5-9

Preface of God the Father
or *Preface of the Epiphany*

www.ingramcontent.com/pod-product-compliance
Ingram Content Group UK Ltd.
Pitfield, Milton Keynes, MK11 3LW, UK
UKHW021846140426
5217IPUK00022B/1617